Power Maths Reception, yearly overview

Summer term

Strand		Unit	Week	Weekly title	Early Learning Goal
Geometry – properties of shape	Unit 12	Exploring patterns	1	Making simple patterns	Children recognise, create and describe patterns.
			2	Exploring more complex patterns	
Number – addition and subtraction	Unit 13	Counting on and counting back	3	Adding by counting on	Using quantities and objects, they add and subtract 2 single-digit numbers and count on or back to find the answer.
			4	Taking away by counting back	
Number – number and place value	Unit 14	Numbers to 20	5	Counting to 20	Children count reliably with numbers from 1 to 20, place them in order.
Number – multiplication and division	Unit 15	Numerical patterns	6	Doubling	They solve problems, including doubling, halving and sharing.
			7	Halving and sharing	
			8	Odds and evens	
Number – number and place value	Unit 16	Measure	9	Length, height and distance	Children use everyday language to talk about size, weight, capacity, position, distance, time and money to compare quantities and objects and to solve problems.
			10	Weight	
			11	Capacity	

Teaching sequence

Power Maths Reception is built around a weekly structure, with each new small step of learning introduced over the course of five lessons. There is enough flexibility in the termly plans to be able to spread out the five lessons over a longer period if you wish, however, we recommend that you work through the materials in the suggested order, as each new concept builds on what has been previously taught.

Each week is introduced in the **Teacher Guide** by an introduction page, which provides practical tips for the week's learning.

The **Learning focus** and **Small steps** help you to understand the key learning for the week and where it fits.

The **Common misconceptions** tells you the likely mistakes children may make and how you can counteract them to ensure children develop a firm understanding.

The **Explore** section provides a bank of ideas for activities you can set up in your classroom throughout the week, helping you to embed the maths concepts into everyday life.

The Introduction page explains the key language, structures and representations that will be introduced in the unit.

Unit 7: Numbers to 10, Week 2: Counting to 6, 7 and 8

Counting to 6, 7 and 8

Learning focus

This week, children learn to count up to 8 objects and show them using concrete representations, including the ten frame. Children are introduced to counters as a representation of an amount for the first time.

Small steps
→ Previous step: Introducing the part-whole model
→ **This step: Counting to 6, 7 and 8**
→ Next step: Counting to 9 and 10

COMMON MISCONCEPTIONS

Children may count too many or too few. Counting the same object more than once is common. They may also repeat a number whilst counting objects or miss a number out. Ask:
- *Can you touch each one as you count it? Can you count again to check your counting?*

When using the ten frame, children may not realise that the counters can be in varying places in the frame, but can still be successfully counted. Ask:
- *Does it matter where the counters are in the ten frame? If you move these counters to here, is there still the same number of counters?*

KEY LANGUAGE

In lesson: one, two, three, four, five, six, seven, eight, 1, 2, 3, 4, 5, 6, 7, 8, **ten frame**, count, how many, same, different, odd one out

Other language to be used by the teacher: more, fewer

STRUCTURES AND REPRESENTATIONS

ten frame, multilink cubes, counters

RESOURCES

Mandatory: ten frame, counters, multilink cubes

Optional: a variety of real-life countable objects (such as building blocks, toy cars or animals), bead strings, paper plates, lolly sticks, pipe cleaners, stick-on eyes, general craft items, boxes, magnifying glass, seeds, plant pots, sticky spots in different colours, marbles, tin, butterfly template (photocopiable 8), ladybird template (photocopiable 9)

EXPLORE

Taking every opportunity throughout the school day to build and reinforce mathematical concepts gives children's learning purpose and meaning in the wider context of their lives.

ACTIVITY	AREA	DESCRIPTION	RESOURCES
Counting legs	Classroom	Provide a selection of model animals and encourage children to sing the song from the **Stimulus** about animals and counting legs.	Model animals
Making spiders	Art area	Make spiders out of paper plates, lolly sticks or pipe cleaners, and stick-on eyes. The spiders should have 8 legs.	Paper plates, lolly sticks, pipe cleaners, stick-on eyes, other craft items
Number detectives	Maths area	Encourage children to collect boxes of a specified number of items (6–8). These items could be hidden around the classroom. Children represent these with counters and on ten frames.	Boxes, counters, magnifying glass, items to collect
Planting seeds	Outside	In small groups, children plant seeds. They can count out up to 8 seeds and plant them outside or into individual plant pots in the classroom. Take a photo and explain that this is the first part of the story (linking back to Unit 5: Time). This can be revisited later when you look at change within 8 to recap *first, then, now*.	Seeds (sunflower or other), plant pots

Day 1: Weekly starter

Check children are secure with prerequisite skills before introducing a new concept.

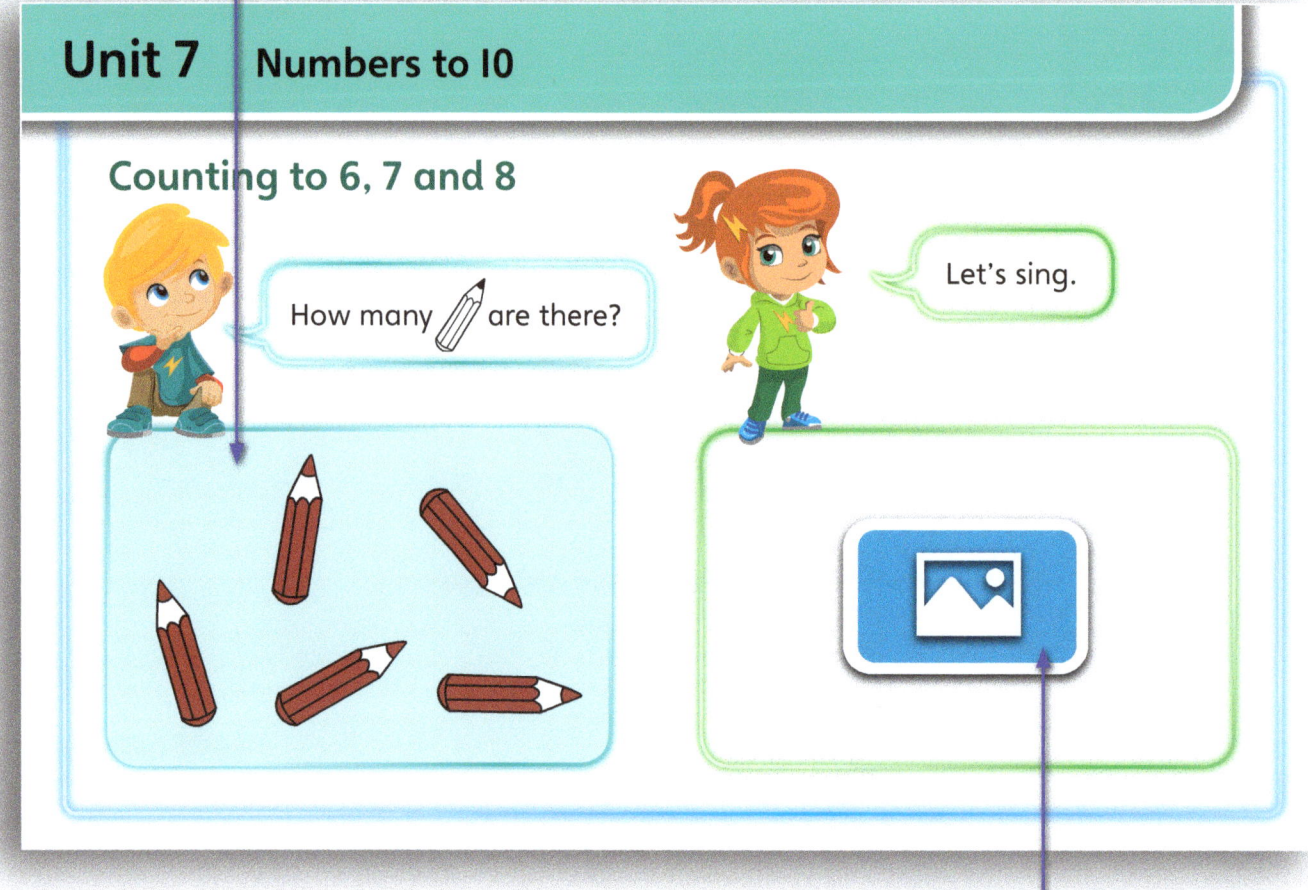

Introduce the week's concept and language by clicking on the hotspot to link to song, story, photograph, picture or game to prompt a practical activity.

Day 2: Discover and Share

Children **Discover** the concept by attempting a practical problem set in a real-life context.

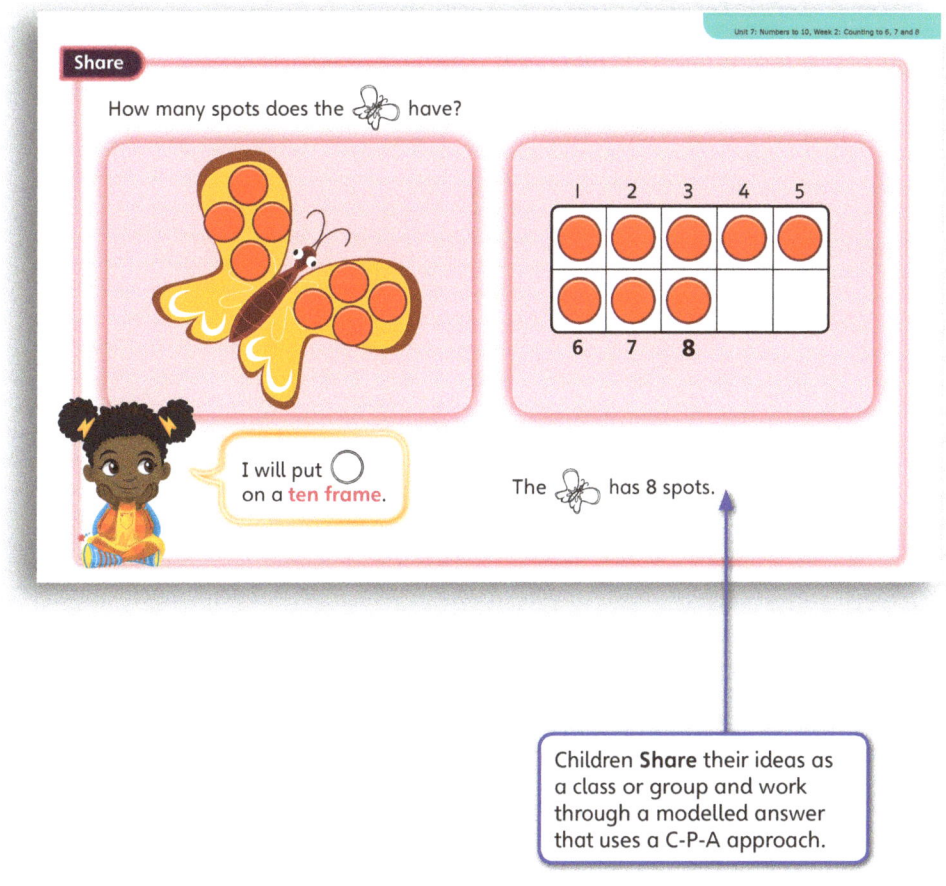

Children **Share** their ideas as a class or group and work through a modelled answer that uses a C-P-A approach.

Day 3: Think together and Practice

Think together provides whole-class guided practice opportunities and moves children on a step in their understanding.

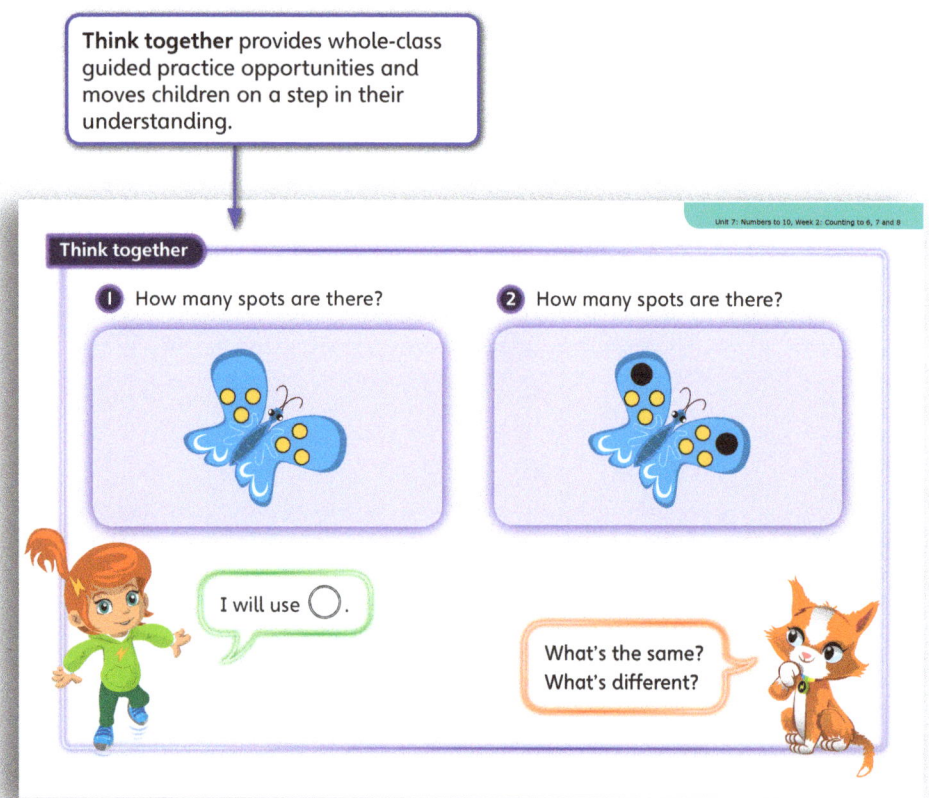

The **Maths Journal** provides an opportunity for independent practice. Children draw, use concrete objects or talk through the problem to show their understanding.

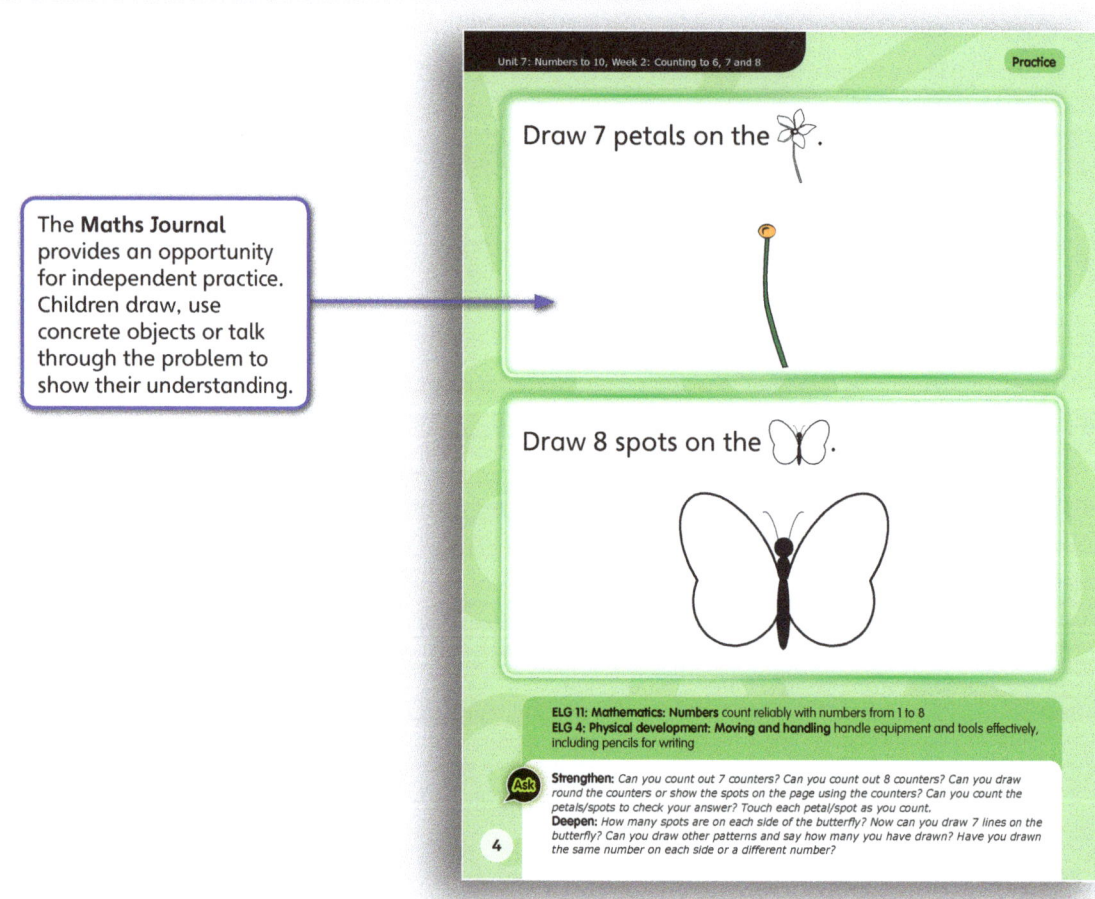

Day 4: Challenge and Strengthen

The whole class attempt the **Challenge**, which deepens children's understanding.

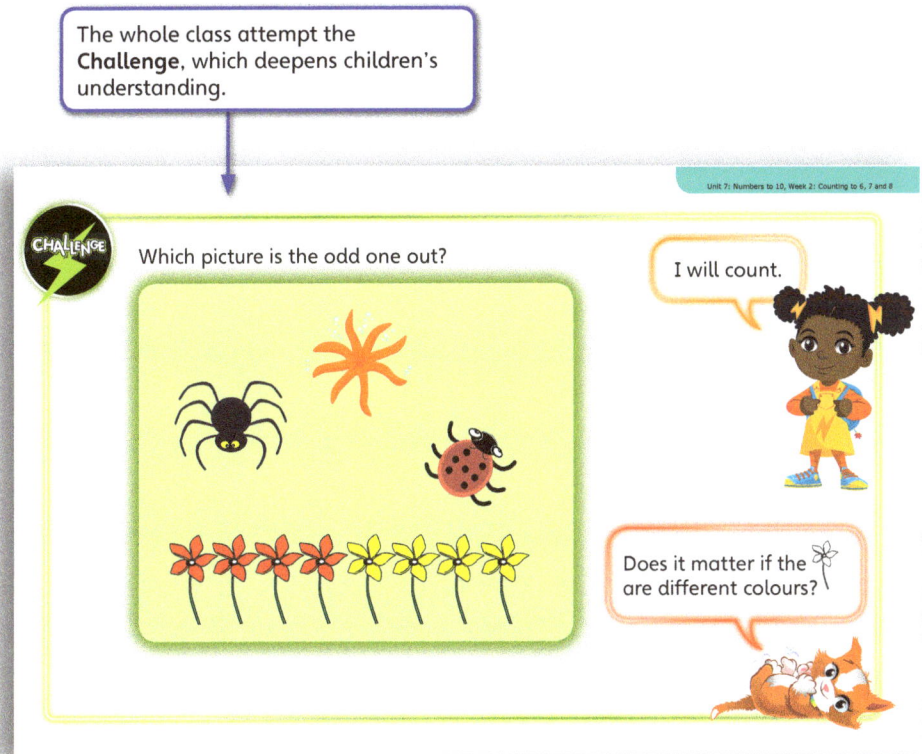

The **Teacher Guide** provides **Strengthen** activity ideas to support those who are not yet ready for the challenge, to help keep the class together.

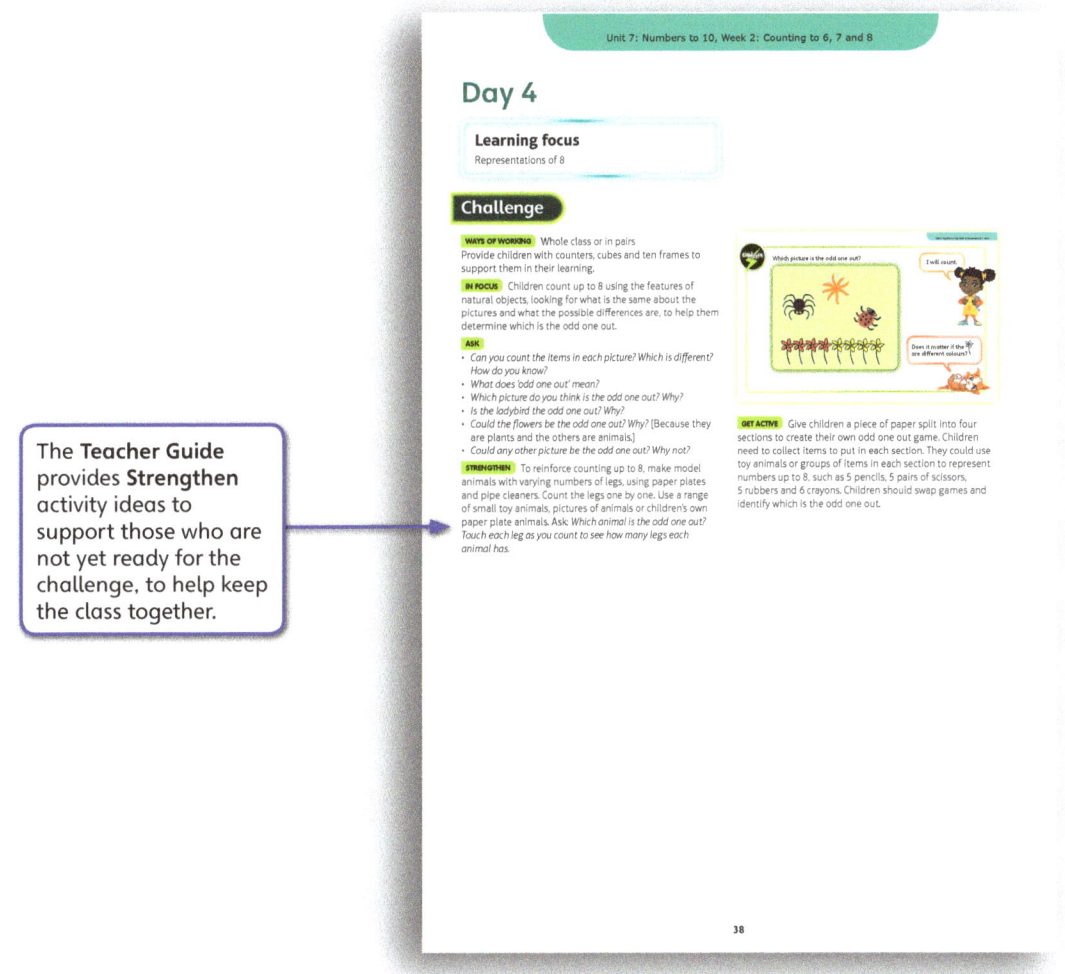

Day 5: Practical activities and Reflect

The **Teacher Guide** suggests practical activities that move children into more abstract maths, such as activities that use sound and movement rather than visual cues.

Children show the depth of their understanding in an open-ended **Reflect** activity in the **Maths Journal**. Children can show whether they have mastered the concept, and they also have the opportunity to demonstrate mastery with greater depth, for example by breaking the whole up in more than one way in the example shown.

Structures and representations

Unlike most other subjects, maths comprises a wide array of abstract concepts – and that is why children and adults so often find it difficult. By taking a Concrete-Pictorial-Abstract (C-P-A) approach, *Power Maths* allows children to tackle concepts in a tangible and more comfortable way.

Non-linear stages

Concrete

Replacing the traditional approach of a teacher working through a problem in front of the class, the concrete stage introduces real objects that children can use to 'do' the maths – any familiar object that a child can manipulate and move to help bring the maths to life. It is important to appreciate, however, that children must always understand the link between models and the objects they represent. For example, children need to first understand that three cakes could be represented by three pretend cakes, and then by three counters or bricks. Frequent practice helps consolidate this essential insight. Although they can be used at any time, good concrete models are an essential first step in understanding.

Pictorial

This stage uses pictorial representations of objects to let children 'see' what particular maths problems look like. It helps them make connections between the concrete and pictorial representations and the abstract maths concept. Children can also create or view a pictorial representation together, enabling discussion and comparisons. The *Power Maths* teaching tools are fantastic for this learning stage, and bar modelling is invaluable for problem solving throughout the primary curriculum.

Abstract

Our ultimate goal is for children to understand abstract mathematical concepts, signs and notation and, of course, some children will reach this stage far more quickly than others. To work with abstract concepts, a child needs to be comfortable with the meaning of, and relationships between, concrete, pictorial and abstract models and representations. The C-P-A approach is not linear, and children may need different types of models at different times. However, when a child demonstrates with concrete models and pictorial representations that they have grasped a concept, we can be confident that they are ready to explore or model it with abstract signs such as numbers and notation.

Use at any time and with any age to support understanding.

Applying the C-P-A approach in Reception

Concrete

Power Maths Reception introduces plenty of opportunities for concrete models in every lesson:

Discover always shows the maths set in a real-life, familiar context. Reception teachers are encouraged to use real, concrete versions of the objects to model the maths when introducing the **Discover** activity wherever possible, or toy versions of the objects. Children should be given the opportunity to handle and manipulate the objects during the **Discover** to help them to see, feel and manipulate the mathematical concepts.

The **Teacher Guide** suggests suitable concrete resources that children can use and manipulate, but you can add in other objects that you have available. Toys such as farm animals or dinosaurs, natural objects such as shells and leaves, and items found in the different classroom areas such as the home corner or sand tray are all great ways to introduce concrete objects into lessons.

If you don't have the suggested object to hand, get creative! Combine it with an art activity to get children to fashion the items out of playdough, such as playdough cakes, or copy and cut out pictures. Anything that gives children a clear link to the problem they are trying to solve, and allows them to physically pick up and move the objects around, will work.

Pictorial

Power Maths Reception introduces pictorial representations following a carefully thought-out progression. Initially, children begin by handling and counting multilink cubes, before learning to use these cubes to represent other things. The key representations introduced are:

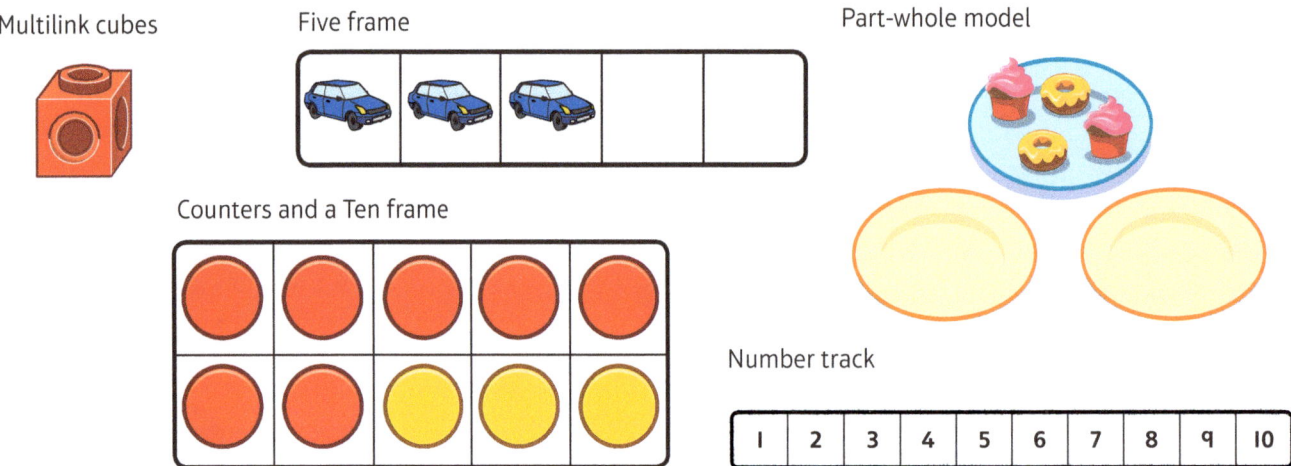

Abstract

Whilst our ultimate goal of children understanding abstract mathematical concepts, signs and notation may seem beyond the scope of Reception, children in the Early Years Foundation Stage can take steps towards building an abstract understanding. *Power Maths Reception* supports children to develop this understanding by:

- Presenting numerals alongside pictorial representations in the modelled answers in **Share** wherever relevant. Teachers should draw children's attention to these numerals during whole-class sessions, and ask children to practise associating the numerals with the numbers they represent.

- Providing large photocopiable numerals at the back of the **Teacher Guide** A (0–5) and **Teacher Guide** B (6–10), so that you can use these to support classroom displays for children to explore.

- Suggesting **Practical activities** towards the end of each week of teaching that begin to reduce children's reliance on visual representation. These activities include applying the maths concepts to sound and movement, meaning that children have to think in a more abstract way about the numbers – for example: *How many claps can you hear? One …[pause] … two, three*. Children are expected to count without relying on having counters or cubes to manipulate, moving them on a step towards more abstract thinking.

The *Power Maths* characters

The *Power Maths* characters model the traits of growth mindset learners and encourage resilience by prompting and questioning children as they work. Appearing frequently in the **Online Flashcards** and **Maths Journals**, they are your allies in teaching and discussion, helping to model methods, alternatives and misconceptions, and to prompt discussion. They encourage and support your children, too: they are all hardworking, enthusiastic and unafraid of making and talking about mistakes.

Meet the team!

Determined Dexter is resolute, resilient and systematic. He concentrates hard, always tries his best and he'll never give up – even though he doesn't always choose the most efficient methods!

Flexible Flo is open-minded and sometimes indecisive. She likes to think differently and come up with a variety of methods or ideas.

'Let's try again.'
'Mistakes are cool!'
'Have I found all of the solutions?'

'Let's try it this way …'
'Can we do it differently?'
'I've got another way of doing this!'

'I'm going to try this!'
'I know how to do that!'
'Want to share my ideas?'

Curious Ash is eager, interested and inquisitive, and he loves solving puzzles and problems. Ash asks lots of questions but sometimes gets distracted.

'What if we tried this …?'
'I wonder …'
'Is there a pattern here?'

Brave Astrid is confident, willing to take risks and unafraid of failure. She is never scared to jump straight into a problem or question, and although she often makes simple mistakes she is happy to talk them through with others.

'Miaow!' **Sparks the Cat**

Mathematical language

Traditionally, we in the UK have tended to try simplifying mathematical language to make it easier for young children to understand. By contrast, evidence and experience show that by diluting the correct language, we actually mask concepts and meanings for children. We then wonder why they are confused by new and different terminology later down the line! *Power Maths* is not afraid of 'hard' words and avoids placing any barriers between children and their understanding of mathematical concepts. As a result, we need to be planned, precise and thorough in building every child's understanding of the language of maths. Throughout the **Teacher Guides** you will find support and guidance on how to introduce new mathematical language to young children.

Use the following key strategies to build children's mathematical vocabulary, understanding and confidence.

Precise and consistent

Everyone in the classroom should use the correct mathematical terms in full, every time. Used consistently, precise maths language will be a familiar and non-threatening part of children's everyday experience.

Full sentences

Teachers and children alike need to use full sentences to explain or respond. When children use complete sentences, it both reveals their understanding and embeds their knowledge.

Stem sentences

These important sentences help children express mathematical concepts accurately, and are used throughout the *Power Maths Reception* resources. Encourage children to repeat them frequently, whether working independently or with others. Examples of stem sentences are:

'4 is a part, 5 is a part, 9 is the whole.'

'There are … groups. There are … in each group.'

Key vocabulary

The unit starters highlight essential vocabulary for every lesson. New terminology is highlighted in bold on the **Online Flashcards** and the **Teacher Guide** lists important mathematical language for every unit and lesson, with new terms flagged in bold, and in the colour of the learning section in which they are introduced, once again.

Make maths part of everyday life

Use every opportunity to build mathematical vocabulary into everyday classroom life. For example, once Time has been introduced, ask children every day what they will do first, then and next today, and encourage them to use words such as *before* and *after*. the more normal you make mathematical language, the less intimidating it becomes.

Keeping the class together

Traditionally, children who learn quickly have been accelerated through the curriculum. As a consequence, their learning may be superficial and will lack the many benefits of enabling children to learn with and from each other.

By contrast, *Power Maths'* mastery approach values real understanding and richer, deeper learning above speed. It sees all children learning the same concept in small, cumulative steps, each finding and mastering challenge at their own level. Remember that when you teach for mastery, EVERYONE can do maths! Those who grasp a concept easily have time to explore and understand that concept at a deeper level. The whole class therefore moves through the curriculum at broadly the same pace via individual learning journeys.

For some teachers, the idea that a whole class can move forward together is revolutionary and challenging. However, the evidence of global good practice clearly shows that this approach drives engagement, confidence, motivation and success for all learners, and not just the high flyers. The strategies below will help you keep your class together on their maths journey.

Strengthen understanding

Use a wide variety of concrete materials to help children strengthen their understanding, and don't be afraid to take more time over a particular topic if you feel your class need it. For example, if *Power Maths Reception* has asked children to count 4 leaves, then set up activities where they need to count 4 pencils, pick out 4 toy cars from a bigger group, hand out 4 snacks, and so on ... anything to help them practise and consolidate their understanding. These activities can be built into everyday classroom life. The **Teacher Guide** provides some ideas for freeflow activities for each week to get you started, as well as **Strengthen** activities you can use as needed.

Deepen understanding

Power Maths Reception lessons offer many opportunities for you to deepen and broaden children's learning. The **Challenge** question each week gives all children an opportunity to explore concepts in greater depth. Children who have grasped concepts quickly should be encouraged to explore alternative solutions, for example, when partitioning a whole of 4 into 1 and 3, what other ways can they break the whole into parts? Could they split the whole into 3 parts? They should also be encouraged to reason and explain why something is true, and how they know they have found all the solutions. **Deepen** activities and questions appear throughout the **Teacher Guide** and in the **Ask** section in the **Maths Journals** to support you in deepening children's understanding.

Prepare to be surprised!

Children may grasp a concept quickly or more slowly. The 'fast graspers' won't always be the same individuals, nor does the speed at which a child understands a concept predict their success in maths. Are they struggling or just working more slowly?

Take cues from the characters

The *Power Maths* characters model mathematical thinking and ideas, and act as prompts for class discussion. They often make suggestions for strategies for tackling a problem as well as asking questions that prompt children to explore the concept in greater depth.

I can use ▢ to help me.

Variation helps visualisation

Children find it much easier to visualise and grasp concepts if they see them presented in a number of ways, so be prepared to offer and encourage many different representations.

For example, the number six could be represented in various ways:

Unit 6
Number bonds within 5

Mastery Expert tip! "Tidy up time is a useful way to consolidate children's understanding of sorting, especially in the home corner. Ask pairs of children to sort a small group of items into two baskets or boxes by a set criteria of colour, shape, size or type."

Don't forget to watch the Exploring composition video!

ELGs

This unit supports the following ELGs:

→ **ELG 12: Mathematics: Shape, space and measures**
explore characteristics of everyday objects and shapes and use mathematical language to describe them

→ **ELG 11: Mathematics: Numbers**
using quantities and objects, add 2 single-digit numbers

WHY THIS UNIT IS IMPORTANT

This unit focuses on number bonds to 5 in the context of a part-whole model. This is the first time children have been introduced to the part-whole model and the idea that there are a limited number of bonds to a given number (5 in this case) and that if 2 and 3, for example, make 5, then so must 3 and 2. This is the basis of understanding addition and subtraction.

WAYS OF WORKING

Have concrete manipulatives, such as real or toy cakes, crayons, balls and ropes or cubes, available for children to recreate the images in the pictures.

WHERE THIS UNIT FITS

→ Unit 4: Change within 5
→ **Unit 6: Number bonds within 5**
→ Unit 7: Numbers to 10

In this unit, children will progress from finding one more and one less within 5 and sorting objects into two groups, to using a part-whole model to represent the groups and the bonds to 5.

Link to Key Stage 1

Number – number and place value
- count to and across 100, forwards and backwards, beginning with 0 or 1, or from any given number; count, read and write numbers to 100 in numerals; count in multiples of twos, fives and tens
- identify and represent numbers using objects and pictorial representations including the number line, and use the language of: equal to, more than, less than (fewer), most, least

Number – addition and subtraction
- represent and use number bonds and related subtraction facts within 20

This unit underpins the KS1 objectives for accurate counting and forms the basis for an understanding of addition and subtraction facts. It also introduces the part-whole model as a way of representing number bonds pictorially.

Unit 6: Number bonds within 5

ASSESSING MASTERY

Children who have mastered this unit will be able to:
- use the language of wholes and parts
- use physical differences and number bonds to 5 to split a whole into two parts.

COMMON MISCONCEPTIONS	STRENGTHENING UNDERSTANDING	GOING DEEPER
When using the vocabulary *whole*, children may confuse the meaning with the word *hole*, as in 'a hole in the ground'.	Use every opportunity to talk about wholes and parts. Ask: *What is the whole of the class?* [All of us.] *What are the parts of the class?* [Each child or group of children, such as those who walk to school and those who do not or the 4-year-olds and 5-year-olds.]	Encourage children to explore the classroom environment to find sets of objects that can be split up into two distinct groups.
When counting the parts in a part-whole model to find the whole, children may include the whole in their count.	Encourage children to count out loud, using concrete manipulatives such as cubes or wooden blocks to represent the whole, and then move them into the separate parts. Ask: *Where is the whole on this model? Where are the parts? How many parts make this whole?*	Encourage children to explore how many different ways sets of up to 5 objects can be split into two parts, then three parts. *Are there still 5 objects?*

STRUCTURES AND REPRESENTATIONS

Part-whole model: This model helps children visualise bonds to 5, understanding that pairs of numbers combine to make a total of 5.

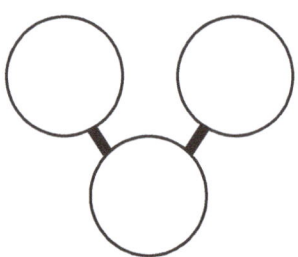

Multilink cubes: Multilink cubes provide a physical representation of an amount, which children can handle and move as they count to support splitting a quantity into two parts.

RESOURCES

Mandatory: multilink cubes, hula hoops

Optional: ball, bowling pins, playdough, candles (in two colours), bean bags, pens, pencils, digit cards

TEACHING TOOLS

part whole

KEY LANGUAGE

There is some key language that children will need to know as part of the learning in this unit.
→ one, two, three, four, five, 1, 2, 3, 4, 5
→ sort, group, **parts**, **whole**, part-whole model
→ how many, count/counting, more than
→ same, different

Unit 6: Number bonds within 5, Week 1: Introducing the part-whole model

Introducing the part-whole model

Learning focus

This week, children will consolidate and build on learning from Unit 2: Sorting. They will be introduced to the vocabulary of *whole* and *part*, and practise the concept of breaking a whole into parts using a part-whole model.

Small steps

→ Previous step: My day
→ **This step: Introducing the part-whole model**
→ Next step: Counting to 6, 7 and 8

COMMON MISCONCEPTIONS

When using the vocabulary *whole*, children may confuse the meaning with the word *hole*, as in 'a hole in the ground'. Ask:
- What is the 'whole' of the class? [All of us.] What are the parts of the class? [Each child or group of children, such as those who walk to school and those who do not or the 4-year-olds and 5-year-olds.]

When counting the parts in a part-whole model to find the whole, children may include the whole in the count. Encourage children to count out loud, using concrete manipulatives such as cubes or wooden blocks to represent the whole and parts. Ask:
- Where is the whole on this model? Where are the parts? How many parts make this whole? Do you need to count the whole as well?

KEY LANGUAGE

In lesson: one, two, three, four, five, 1, 2, 3, 4, 5, sort, group, whole, parts, how many, counting

Other language to be used by the teacher: part-whole model, count, same, different, more than

STRUCTURES AND REPRESENTATIONS

part-whole models, multilink cubes

RESOURCES

Mandatory: multilink cubes, hula hoops

Optional: balls, bowling pins, playdough, candles (in two colours), bean bags, hoop, pens, pencils, skipping ropes, digit cards

EXPLORE

Taking every opportunity throughout the school day to build and reinforce mathematical concepts gives children's learning purpose and meaning in the wider context of their lives.

ACTIVITY	AREA	DESCRIPTION	RESOURCES
Bowling	Inside or outside space	Set up a bowling activity using up to 5 items. Ask children to partition the items that are left standing and those that fall over. Spark discussion about the whole and the parts.	Ball, bowling pins
Playdough birthday cakes	Messy play area	Make sets of up to 5 playdough cakes, decorating each cake with one candle, using two different colours of candle. Encourage children to draw or complete part-whole models to show the two colours.	Playdough, sets of candles in two colours
Bean bag throwing	Inside or outside space	Choose a small number of bean bags (up to 5). Ask children to attempt to throw all 5 bean bags into a hula hoop. Next, ask children to count how many land in the hoop and how many miss. Ask: *How many bean bags did you start with? How many landed in the hoop? How many missed? How can you sort the bean bags into two groups or parts?*	Bean bags, hula hoop

Unit 6: Number bonds within 5, Week 1: Introducing the part-whole model

Day 1

Learning focus
Sorting objects into two groups

Before you teach
- Are all children able to count to 5 confidently?
- Can children confidently sort a small group of objects into two groups?
- Are children confident using sorting vocabulary such as *more*, *fewer*, *same* and *different*?

Starter

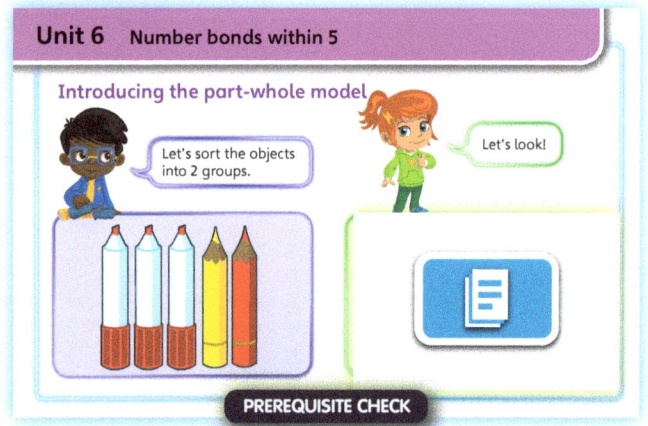
PREREQUISITE CHECK

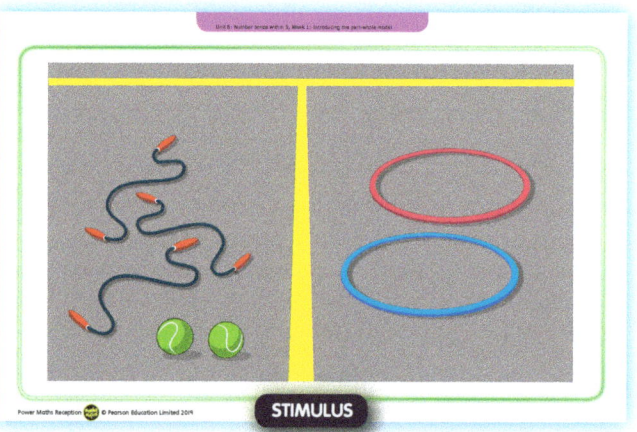
STIMULUS

PREREQUISITE CHECK Sorting felt-tipped pens and pencil crayons into two groups.

WAYS OF WORKING Whole class

Where possible, give children access to pens and pencils, encouraging them to physically sort them into two parts, and then back into a whole.

IN FOCUS This **Prerequisite check** practises the Unit 2 skill of sorting using the properties of objects. Children can sort by pens and pencils (the more obvious grouping) or by colour (more difficult to spot).

ASK
- Can you remember what 'sort' means?
- What objects are shown here?
- Which item are there more of? Which item are there fewer of?
- How could you sort them into two groups?
- What colours are they? Is there another way to sort them?

STIMULUS Picture to prompt a guided activity
The picture shows objects and empty hoops as an introduction to the parts in a part-whole model.

WAYS OF WORKING Whole class or small groups

Spark children's interest with the **Stimulus** activity. Encourage children to discuss how to sort the objects into two parts (the hoops), anticipating the layout of a part-whole model that they will be introduced to in the **Discover** activity.

IN FOCUS The focus of the **Stimulus** is to move children towards the mathematical skill of sorting objects into hoops, a precursor to the part-whole model. Another important step here is the introduction of the language of *parts* and *whole*.

Encourage mastery of the concepts of parts and wholes by using every opportunity to identify a whole and its parts in everyday contexts, and how parts can go back together to make the whole, and then break up again to go back into parts. Use the **Explore** table on page 26 for more activity ideas to help embed the learning.

ASK
- Look at the picture. What can you see?
- What might the two parts be? Where could you put the two parts to make this clear?
- [After deciding how to sort the parts.] *If these are the parts, what is the whole? And if you break them up again into two groups, what are the parts?*

GET ACTIVE Use the picture to lead into a guided activity in the outside area. Lay hula hoops on the floor in the shape of a part-whole model (1 hoop at the top, 2 hoops below). Place 3 skipping ropes and 2 balls in the *whole* hoop. Guide children towards sorting the items into the two *part* hoops, using the **Ask** questions above as a starting point if necessary.

27

Unit 6: Number bonds within 5, Week 1: Introducing the part-whole model

Day 2

Learning focus

Sorting a whole into two distinct parts

Discover

WAYS OF WORKING Whole class or small groups
Have concrete manipulatives, such as real or toy cakes or cubes, available for children to recreate the cakes in the **Discover** picture. Circular plates would be useful to support children's sorting of the cakes.

IN FOCUS The focus of this activity is to show how a whole (5 cakes) can be sorted into two parts (two types of cake). Guide the discussion about how the whole can be sorted into two parts, to consolidate the key language of *whole* and *parts*. Use every opportunity to embed this language, modelling stem sentences for children to copy, such as: *You sorted the cakes by moving them into two parts, now put them back together to show the whole again.*

ASK
- *What can you see in the picture?*
- *What are the parts? How many cupcakes are there? How many doughnuts are there?*
- *How many cakes are there altogether? What is the whole?*
- *How many doughnuts will Aidan's toy get? How many cupcakes will Ella's toy get?*

STRENGTHEN Use stem sentences to support understanding of where the whole and the two parts are, for example: *The **whole** is ...* [all of the cakes]. *The **parts** are ...* [the two plates of cakes]. *One part is the plate of ...* [2 doughnuts] *and the other part is the ...* [plate of 3 cupcakes]. Children can use cubes in different colours to represent the two types of cake and use real plates or hoops to physically sort them.

Share

WAYS OF WORKING Whole class

IN FOCUS Children can use concrete manipulatives to help sort the cakes. The part-whole model shows how the whole number of 5 cakes can be sorted and split into two distinct parts. The **Discover** picture can be recreated using the **Part whole teaching tool**, using two colours of counters or cubes to represent the cakes. Show the items moving from the whole to the parts and back again.

ASK
- *Where is the whole? Where are the parts?*
- *What has happened to the whole in the second picture?*

STRENGTHEN Provide children with the opportunity to manipulate physical blocks or cubes, moving them from the whole into two separate parts as you work through the **Share** activity. Demonstrate how the whole is empty when it has been split into the two parts, reinforcing how the whole becomes two parts.

DEEPEN Children can make their own teddy bears' picnic using 4–6 cubes or building blocks in two different colours and two different sizes to represent cakes. Encourage children to split the 'cakes' up in different ways between two

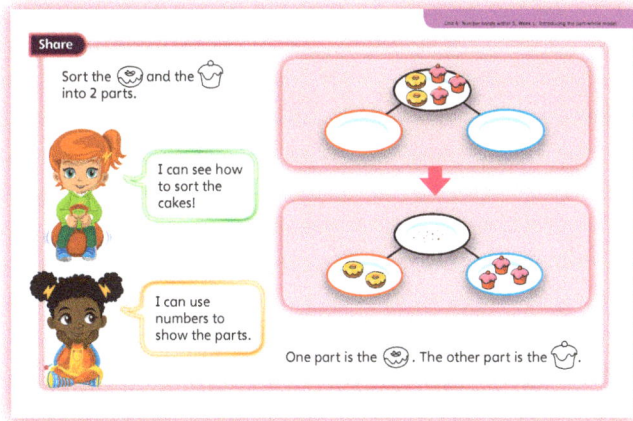

plates. Ask them to show this on a part-whole model using drawings or refer them to what Flo says and encourage them to use digit cards.

GET ACTIVE Ask children to make sets of up to 5 playdough cakes, decorating each cake with one candle, using two different colours of candle. Encourage them to draw or complete part-whole models to show the two colours, thinking about ways they can sort the cakes they make.

28

Unit 6: Number bonds within 5, Week 1: Introducing the part-whole model

Day 3

Learning focus
Recognising different representations of two parts

Think together

WAYS OF WORKING Whole class or small groups
Have cubes or blocks in two different colours available for children to use to represent the cakes.

IN FOCUS The focus of this **Think Together** activity is on becoming familiar with the concept of wholes and parts. Use the **Ask** questions to spark discussion and consolidate understanding. The small step of progression between the questions is moving children from sorting different items to sorting identical items, challenging them to look for different ways to sort.

ASK

- Question ❶: *What is the same and what is different? What is the whole? How many parts do you need to sort into? What could the parts be?*
- Question ❷: *Are there any other ways to sort the cakes?*

STRENGTHEN Children who are not yet ready to move onto concrete representations should be encouraged to use toy cakes or playdough cakes to represent the problem.

Use the **Part whole teaching tool** to reinforce number bonds to 5. Move 4 counters into the whole and then move 3 counters from the whole to one of the parts. Next move

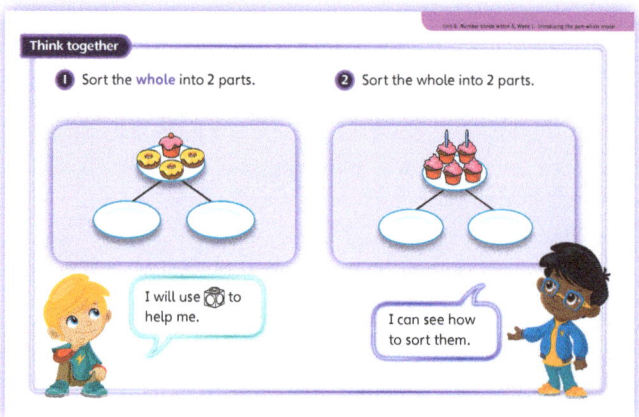

the remaining 1 counter from the whole into the other part and explain to children what you are doing. Use complete sentences to model answers for children to repeat. Ask them to say their own sentences based on the number facts you display on the teaching tool.

DEEPEN Encourage children to think more deeply about the meaning of the words *whole* and *parts*. Ask: *What is the whole here? Will the whole stay the same if you swap the two parts? Is there another way to show the parts? Can you explain your answer?*

Practice: Journal 1

WAYS OF WORKING Independent thinking

IN FOCUS The focus of this **Practice** activity is to reinforce the vocabulary of *whole* and *parts* and to embed understanding of these concepts, and of the part-whole model, using plates as a more familiar, natural context.

MASTERY CHECKPOINT Children who have mastered this concept can say how they know what the whole is and what the parts are, and can show this using cubes or blocks, or by drawing in their journals. When prompted, they can explore different ways of splitting the whole and they can explain that the whole does not change, even if you move the parts.

29

Unit 6: Number bonds within 5, Week 1: Introducing the part-whole model

Day 4

Learning focus

Finding different ways to sort groups into parts

Challenge

WAYS OF WORKING Whole class or in pairs

Guide children who need more support, using cubes or blocks to represent the biscuits. Prompt thinking using the **Ask** questions. Some children may find it helpful to work in pairs. Use the **Part whole teaching tool** to model physically breaking a whole of 5 into parts.

IN FOCUS In this **Challenge**, all the items in the picture are identical so that children need to choose how to split them without the support of having obvious groups. Without any physical differences, children now attempt to sort the biscuits by amount, using their knowledge of number bonds to 5. Encourage children to discover for themselves that there is more than one way to sort the whole into parts, for example, 1 and 4, 2 and 3, etc.

ASK

- What is the whole? What is the same? Can you see any differences? How else could you break the whole into parts?
- Is there more than one way to do this? How will you find out? What could you use to help you?
- How do you know that there is more than one way? Work with a partner to find all the ways.

STRENGTHEN Work closely with children who need more support attempting this **Challenge**, ensuring they have access to concrete manipulatives that they can physically move to represent different number bonds to 5. Encourage children to count out loud as they work.

DEEPEN The **Challenge** question has purposefully not guided children to breaking the whole into a specific number of parts, but has left the number of parts to split the whole into as an open question. Children who have fully mastered the concept may be able to suggest the idea of separating the whole into more than two parts. Encourage them to try this, and ask questions such as: *What is the whole? What are the parts? Is there another way you could do this? What happens if you break the whole into three parts? Does the whole stay the same, no matter how many parts you break it into?*

Unit 6: Number bonds within 5, Week 1: Introducing the part-whole model

Day 5

Learning focus
Finding number bonds to 3, 4 and 5

Practical activities

WAYS OF WORKING Whole class

IN FOCUS This activity builds on recognising and identifying the parts and the whole and encouraging children as much as possible to use the language of *whole* and *parts* when describing what they are doing. Prompt children with stem sentences from the **Online Flashcard** as much as possible to reinforce the accurate use of this key language. For example: *The whole is … the parts are …*

GET ACTIVE Hoops
Outside or in the hall, put hula hoops on the ground laid out like a part-whole model; one hoop at the top and two hoops below. Ask a group of 5 children to stand in the 'whole' hoop. Ask the other children to suggest how they could be split into two parts (long hair or short hair, age 4 or age 5). Ask the 5 children to split the group into the two parts suggested. Repeat with a different group of 5 children, using different criteria for the split. Split the class into groups of 3, 4 or 5 children. Ask them to count how many are in their group. Prompt thinking with questions, such as: *Is that the whole or the part? How can you divide your group into two parts? How many children is the whole for your group?* Ask children to stand in the two hoops that represent the two parts of their whole. Encourage them to use stem sentences: *The whole is 4; the parts are 2 and 2*. Use every opportunity to describe what they are doing, to help embed this key language of *whole* and *parts*.

Reflect: Journal 2

WAYS OF WORKING Independent thinking

IN FOCUS As in the **Challenge** activity, this **Reflect** activity focuses on sorting a whole when all the parts are identical, requiring children to break the whole using number bonds to 4 – for example, 3 in one part, 1 in the other part – and prompting children to find all possible number bonds to 4. Children are not guided towards two parts, so the possibilities of ways to sort the parts are much greater, giving opportunity for broader and more creative thinking. Children may need to be told that they are allowed to break the whole into more than two parts.

MASTERY CHECKPOINT **Children who have mastered this concept** can confidently use the language of *whole* and *parts* and can use physical differences and number bonds to 5 to split a whole into two parts.

Children who have not yet mastered this concept need support and prompts to break a whole into two parts.

Children who have mastered this concept with greater depth can show all the ways of splitting the whole into parts (possibly including using more than two parts) and can explain, when prompted, how they know this.

Unit 7
Numbers to 10

Mastery Expert tip! "When teaching this unit, I used the contexts given in the pictures to make the maths as practical as possible. The children were far more confident about explaining their ideas when we used actual or toy items or their own collections of objects. They loved making their own resources in the art area to use in our Maths lessons."

Don't forget to watch the Counting skills video!

ELGs

This unit supports the following ELGs:

→ **ELG 11: Mathematics: Numbers**
count reliably with numbers from 1 to 20, place them in order and say which number is one more or one less than a given number

→ **ELG 4: Physical development: Moving and handling**
handle equipment and tools effectively, including pencils for writing

WHY THIS UNIT IS IMPORTANT

This unit focuses on children's ability to recognise, represent and manipulate numbers to 10. Children begin by counting groups of objects up to 6, 7 and 8, before moving on to 9 and 10. Children will learn to recognise and count different representations of numbers up to 10 and use a ten frame to help structure their counting and reasoning. The concept of cardinality is reinforced throughout and children are encouraged to subitise and to see number bonds beyond 5 as an efficient counting strategy.

WAYS OF WORKING

Make sure there are plenty of ten frames and counters for children to use alongside the **Online Flashcards** in this unit. Ensure you have a box of buttons for the Week 3 **Starter** and toy or actual objects to represent the items in the pictures.

WHERE THIS UNIT FITS

→ Unit 6: Number bonds within 5

→ **Unit 7: Numbers to 10**

→ Unit 8: Comparing numbers within 10

In this unit, children count to 10 and represent numbers using concrete and pictorial representations. The ten frame and counters are used for the first time and the concept of number bonds is explored.

Link to Key Stage 1

Number – number and place value

- count to and across 100, forwards and backwards, beginning with 0 or 1, or from any given number; count, read and write numbers to 100 in numerals; count in multiples of twos, fives and tens
- identify and represent numbers using objects and pictorial representations including the number line, and use the language of: equal to, more than, less than (fewer), most, least

The learning in this unit establishes methods of counting objects reliably and introduces the ten frame and the concept that numbers can be shown in different representations, including real life (concrete) items such as spots on a butterfly, pictorially as cubes or counters and as an abstract numeral.

Unit 7: Numbers to 10

ASSESSING MASTERY

Children who have mastered this unit will be able to:
- count numbers up to 10 using one-to-one correspondence
- represent the numbers 6–10 on a ten frame
- start to recognise that they can count on using a ten frame, understanding that a full row is 5
- count 6–10 objects out from a larger group

COMMON MISCONCEPTIONS	STRENGTHENING UNDERSTANDING	GOING DEEPER
Children may find counting backwards trickier, missing out numbers and saying them in the wrong order.	Role-play situations where counting down is necessary, such as a rocket launch or blowing out birthday candles. Also sing songs like 'Ten green bottles', 'Ten little monkeys' or 'Ten speckled frogs'.	Count forwards in a circle of up to 10 children. When the teacher shakes a tambourine switch to counting backwards.
Children may count too many or too few. They may count an object more than once or miss one out.	Encourage children to line up objects in a row as they count and touch each object as they count.	Challenge children to count up to 10 objects from a larger group. Do they know when to stop counting?

STRUCTURES AND REPRESENTATIONS

Ten frame: The ten frame helps children visualise 10. It will also help strengthen children's fluency with numbers up to 10, demonstrating how they can be arranged in different ways but still be worth the same amount.

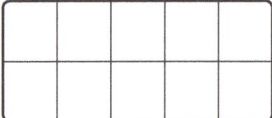

Multilink cubes: Multilink cubes provide a physical representation of an amount, which children can handle and move as they count and compare.

Counters: Counters are used for the first time to represent objects being counted. They can be placed in the ten frame or lined up in a row.

RESOURCES

Mandatory: ten frame (photocopiable 6), counters, multilink cubes, box of buttons

Optional: a variety of real-life countable objects (blocks, toy cars or animals), bead strings, paper plates, lolly sticks, pipe cleaners, stick-on eyes, general craft items, boxes, magnifying glass, seeds, plant pots, sticky spots in different colours, marbles, tin, large dice, digit cards, containers, hula hoops, bean bags, glue, card, transparent containers, small objects, plates, cups, butterfly template (photocopiable 8), ladybird template (photocopiable 9), action cards (photocopiable 10)

TEACHING TOOLS

ten frame

KEY LANGUAGE

There is some key language that children will need to know as part of the learning in this unit:
- one, two, three, four, five, six, seven, eight, nine, ten, 1, 2, 3, 4, 5, 6, 7, 8, 9, 10
- **ten frame**, count, how many, total, altogether
- count forwards, count backwards
- same, different, odd one out
- more, fewer, collections, group
- dice, method

Unit 7: Numbers to 10, Week 2: Counting to 6, 7 and 8

Counting to 6, 7 and 8

Learning focus
This week, children learn to count up to 8 objects and show them using concrete representations, including the ten frame. Children are introduced to counters as a representation of an amount for the first time.

Small steps
→ Previous step: Introducing the part-whole model
→ **This step: Counting to 6, 7 and 8**
→ Next step: Counting to 9 and 10

COMMON MISCONCEPTIONS
Children may count too many or too few. Counting the same object more than once is common. They may also repeat a number whilst counting objects or miss a number out. Ask:
- *Can you touch each one as you count it? Can you count again to check your counting?*

When using the ten frame, children may not realise that the counters can be in varying places in the frame, but can still be successfully counted. Ask:
- *Does it matter where the counters are in the ten frame? If you move these counters to here, is there still the same number of counters?*

KEY LANGUAGE
In lesson: one, two, three, four, five, six, seven, eight, 1, 2, 3, 4, 5, 6, 7, 8, **ten frame**, count, how many, same, different, odd one out

Other language to be used by the teacher: more, fewer

STRUCTURES AND REPRESENTATIONS
ten frame, multilink cubes, counters

RESOURCES
Mandatory: ten frame, counters, multilink cubes

Optional: a variety of real-life countable objects (such as building blocks, toy cars or animals), bead strings, paper plates, lolly sticks, pipe cleaners, stick-on eyes, general craft items, boxes, magnifying glass, seeds, plant pots, sticky spots in different colours, marbles, tin, butterfly template (photocopiable 8), ladybird template (photocopiable 9)

EXPLORE
Taking every opportunity throughout the school day to build and reinforce mathematical concepts gives children's learning purpose and meaning in the wider context of their lives.

ACTIVITY	AREA	DESCRIPTION	RESOURCES
Counting legs	Classroom	Provide a selection of model animals and encourage children to sing the song from the **Stimulus** about animals and counting legs.	Model animals
Making spiders	Art area	Make spiders out of paper plates, lolly sticks or pipe cleaners, and stick-on eyes. The spiders should have 8 legs.	Paper plates, lolly sticks, pipe cleaners, stick-on eyes, other craft items
Number detectives	Maths area	Encourage children to collect boxes of a specified number of items (6–8). These items could be hidden around the classroom. Children represent these with counters and on ten frames.	Boxes, counters, magnifying glass, items to collect
Planting seeds	Outside	In small groups, children plant seeds. They can count out up to 8 seeds and plant them outside or into individual plant pots in the classroom. Take a photo and explain that this is the first part of the story (linking back to Unit 5: Time). This can be revisited later when you look at change within 8 to recap *first, then, now*.	Seeds (sunflower or other), plant pots

Unit 7: Numbers to 10, Week 2: Counting to 6, 7 and 8

Day 1

Learning focus
Counting to 8

Before you teach

- What resources will you provide for children who find counting from a picture more difficult?
- How will you provide scaffolding to build up children's ability to relate amounts of concrete materials and abstract numbers to one another?
- Are all children able to make numbers they are familiar with on the five frame?

Starter

PREREQUISITE CHECK

PREREQUISITE CHECK Counting 5 pencils displayed in various orientations.

WAYS OF WORKING Whole class
Provide real pencils for children to recreate the image and line up the pencils to count them.

IN FOCUS This **Prerequisite check** practises the Unit 1 skill of counting to 5 accurately.

ASK
- Can you remember how to count?
- Which number do you start the count with?
- What could help you to count accurately?
- How can you check that you have counted correctly?

Animal legs
I am an ant.   I am a spider.
[Children repeat.]   [Children repeat.]
Let's count my legs.   Let's count my legs.
[Children repeat.]   [Children repeat.]
I've got 1 and 2, 3 and 4,   I've got 1 and 2, 3 and 4,
5 and 6. SIX!   5 and 6, 7 and 8. EIGHT!
I am an ant.   I am a spider.
[Children repeat.]   [Children repeat.]
I've got six legs!   I've got eight legs!
[Children repeat.]   [Children repeat.]

STIMULUS

STIMULUS Song: Animal legs
Introduce the song to children.
The song can be repeated with different animals including scorpion (8 legs), beetle (6 legs), horse (4 legs), human (2 legs).

WAYS OF WORKING Whole class
Provide children with toy animals to sing the song about. They should touch the legs of the animals as they count.

IN FOCUS Play the **Stimulus** song to encourage children to count forwards to 8. Once the song has been modelled by the teacher, other children can take the lead in the song whilst the rest of the class repeats the lines.

The song will encourage children to think about different animals and use their counting for a purpose to count the total number of legs. Children may be excited to share their favourite animal and how many legs it has.

ASK
- Which animals have 4 legs?
- How many legs does a spider have?
- Can you think of another animal you could sing about?
- Can anyone think of an animal with 3, 5 or 7 legs?
- Which creature has more legs, a spider or an ant?

GET ACTIVE When children are singing, encourage them to show the numbers they are saying on their fingers one by one. Children could also create different actions for each animal that they are singing about.

35

Unit 7: Numbers to 10, Week 2: Counting to 6, 7 and 8

Day 2

Learning focus
Cardinality to 8

Discover

WAYS OF WORKING Whole class or small groups

IN FOCUS Children use the **Discover** picture to count the different features of the creatures (legs, spots).

ASK
- *How many spots does the butterfly have? Can you point to each spot as you count?*
- *What can you use to represent the spots? How many have you got altogether?*
- *How else could you represent the spots? What can you use to help you count?*

STRENGTHEN Use the butterfly template (photocopiable 8) and draw the spots shown in the picture on the butterfly. Encourage children to touch each spot as they count then to put a counter on top of each spot, counting again to check.

DEEPEN Ask: *What else can you see on the picture? Can you count anything else?* Children might link back to counting

legs on the animals or they may count the spots on the ladybird. Encourage children to discuss their favourite animals and bugs. How many legs do they each have?

Share

WAYS OF WORKING Whole class

IN FOCUS For the first time, children use counters to support their counting to 8 and a ten frame to represent the number of spots. Remind children of the five frame, introduced in Term A, discussing what is the same and what is different about the ten frame. Children could begin by counting out up to 8 counters then placing them on the ten frame in any order. They compare their ten frame with a partner's. Discuss what is the same and what is different about the way the counters have been placed. Use the **Ten frame teaching tool** to model moving counters onto a ten frame.

ASK
- *Can you point to and say each number aloud as you count? How many spots are there altogether?*
- *Do you need to count all the counters on the ten frame? Can you see that 8 is 5 and 3 more?*
- *Does it matter which spaces you fill in on the ten frame? Could you have used the ten frame in a different way?*

STRENGTHEN Encourage children to practise using the ten frame by counting the number of spots on the ladybird in the **Discover** picture. Provide children with a ladybird template (photocopiable 9) for them to add the spots to, using counters, which they can then transfer onto a ten frame.

DEEPEN Draw children's attention to the numerals around the ten frame. Ask if they can read them. Encourage children

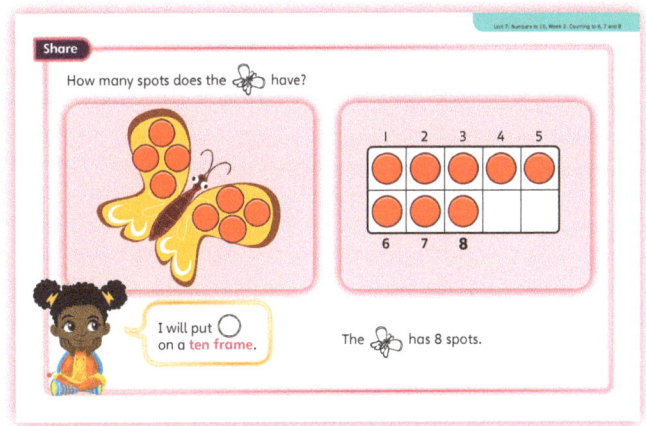

to use counters and a ten frame to show all the things they can count in the **Discover** picture. Does it matter where the empty spaces are in the ten frame? [No.] Sing the **Stimulus** song again and ask children to lead the singing by singing the first line by themselves or even introducing new creatures into the song.

GET ACTIVE Encourage children to use the butterfly template (photocopiable 8) and place up to 8 counters on it. Children work in pairs, asking their partner to count how many there are altogether. Children can challenge each other to count the counters on the butterfly and place them on a ten frame.

36

Unit 7: Numbers to 10, Week 2: Counting to 6, 7 and 8

Day 3

Learning focus
Counting different representations up to 8

Think together

WAYS OF WORKING Whole class
Ensure coloured pencils, counters and ten frames are available for children to use. Use the **Ten frame teaching tool** to represent the spots on a ten frame.

IN FOCUS In Question ①, children count 6 spots on a butterfly. Question ② repeats this image with the addition of 2 larger spots in a different colour, so that children realise that objects do not have to be the same size or colour to be in the same count. They consider what is the same and what is different about the two pictorial representations. This will move them towards seeing how 8 can be made up of smaller numbers, 6 and 2, which prepares them for learning number bonds to 10 later on.

ASK
- Question ①: *How many spots are there altogether? Can you point to each spot as you count? How many spots are on each side? Do you need to use counters to help you count?*
- Question ①: *Can you count the number of spots without pointing to them? Can you count in your head?*
- Question ②: *In what way is this butterfly the same as the other one? Which spots are in the same place? Can you start counting at 6 and count on to find how many there are altogether? Can you show this on a ten frame?*

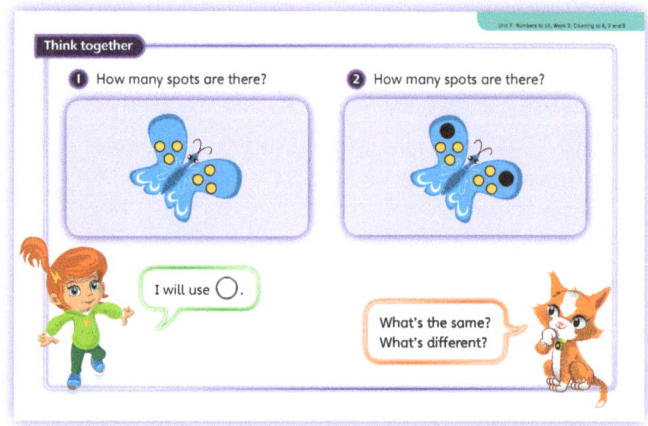

- Question ②: *How is this butterfly different? Does it matter that the spots are a different size and colour?*

STRENGTHEN Use the butterfly template (photocopiable 8) and a dice and provide a selection of coloured sticky spots. Children choose a colour, roll the dice and put that number of spots on the butterfly. Children choose a different colour and roll again.

DEEPEN Give children a ten frame and 8 counters. Ask: *How many different ways can you show 8 on the ten frame?*

Practice: Journal 1

WAYS OF WORKING Independent thinking

IN FOCUS Children draw 7 petals on a flower and 8 spots on a butterfly. Children can print the petals and spots or draw around counters for support. They can also be challenged to draw different amounts of things onto their flower and butterfly, such as 5 yellow spots, 7 red spots, 6 blue lines or 8 leaves.

MASTERY CHECKPOINT Check that children have drawn the right number of petals and spots. Are they able to represent other numbers in different ways? Check that children can count out 7 and then 8 counters and represent each on a ten frame. Can they represent them in more than one way?

37

Unit 7: Numbers to 10, Week 2: Counting to 6, 7 and 8

Day 4

Learning focus
Representations of 8

Challenge

WAYS OF WORKING Whole class or in pairs
Provide children with counters, cubes and ten frames to support them in their learning.

IN FOCUS Children count up to 8 using the features of natural objects, looking for what is the same about the pictures and what the possible differences are, to help them determine which is the odd one out.

ASK
- Can you count the items in each picture? Which is different? How do you know?
- What does 'odd one out' mean?
- Which picture do you think is the odd one out? Why?
- Is the ladybird the odd one out? Why?
- Could the flowers be the odd one out? Why? [Because they are plants and the others are animals.]
- Could any other picture be the odd one out? Why not?

STRENGTHEN To reinforce counting up to 8, make model animals with varying numbers of legs, using paper plates and pipe cleaners. Count the legs one by one. Use a range of small toy animals, pictures of animals or children's own paper plate animals. Ask: Which animal is the odd one out? Touch each leg as you count to see how many legs each animal has.

GET ACTIVE Give children a piece of paper split into four sections to create their own odd one out game. Children need to collect items to put in each section. They could use toy animals or groups of items in each section to represent numbers up to 8, such as 5 pencils, 5 pairs of scissors, 5 rubbers and 6 crayons. Children should swap games and identify which is the odd one out.

Unit 7: Numbers to 10, Week 2: Counting to 6, 7 and 8

Day 5

Learning focus
Counting to 8 using abstraction

Practical activities

WAYS OF WORKING Whole class
You will need a large jar of marbles and a tin for this activity.

IN FOCUS Children count the number of marbles by listening to the sound of each one being dropped into a tin, which encourages thinking of numbers as an abstract concept as well as an amount they can physically count. Children can check their answer by counting the marbles using one-to-one correspondence. Children also count backwards to count the marbles back out of the tin.

GET ACTIVE Counting marbles
Drop 7 marbles slowly into a tin, one at time. Ask: *How many marbles do you think are in the tin? How do you know? Can you check by counting the marbles out of the tin?* Next, count out the marbles in front of children. You could give one marble each to a child so they can see that there are 7 altogether. Put the marbles back into the tin, counting them in carefully together. Now take them out, one at a time, starting with 7, and counting backwards from 7 down to 0. Say: *There are none left in the tin.* Adapt the game by dropping different amounts of marbles into the tin (up to and including 8) and then counting them back out.

Reflect: Journal 2

WAYS OF WORKING Independent thinking

IN FOCUS Children bring all their learning around the number 8 together to represent 8 in multiple ways. Encourage children to use the ten frame to show 8 in different ways. Remind children about the different ways they have shown 8 throughout the week. Prompt them to think about abstraction, too. Ask: *Are 8 claps still 8, even if there's nothing to see or touch? Can you think of any different ways to show 8?*

MASTERY CHECKPOINT **Children who have mastered this concept** can represent 8 using counters and a ten frame. They can count forwards to 8 and identify numbers up to 8 by counting.

Children who have not yet mastered this concept can represent 8 using counters and a ten frame with support. They are starting to count objects independently, touching each object as they count.

Children who have mastered this concept with greater depth can represent 8 on a ten frame in various ways. They can count forwards and backwards to 8 independently. They can identify numbers up to 8 by counting and are starting to count in their head and subitise smaller amounts.

Unit 7: Numbers to 10, Week 3: Counting to 9 and 10

Counting to 9 and 10

Learning focus
This week, children will learn to count to 10. They will be introduced to the numbers 9 and 10 and use the ten frame to scaffold their counting to 10.

Small steps
→ Previous step: Counting to 6, 7 and 8
→ **This step: Counting to 9 and 10**
→ Next step: Comparing groups up to 10

COMMON MISCONCEPTIONS

Children may count too few or too many. Counting the same object more than once is common. Children should be encouraged to line up objects when counting and touch each object as they count. Ask:
- *Have you counted carefully? Can you check by counting again slowly?*

Children may think that objects need to be in a single row to be countable. Show 6–10 counters in one row, then move them into two rows as represented on a ten frame. Ask:
- *How many counters are there in this row? How many counters are there now? How many counters fill this part of the ten frame?*

KEY LANGUAGE

In lesson: 1, 2, 3, 4, 5, 6, 7, 8, 9, 10, one, two, three, four, five, six, seven, eight, nine, ten, how many, count, group, same, different, totals

Other language to be used by the teacher: collections, altogether, ten frame, dice, method

STRUCTURES AND REPRESENTATIONS

ten frame, multilink cubes, counters

RESOURCES

Mandatory: ten frame, counters, multilink cubes, box of buttons

Optional: 1–10 bead string, large dice, digit cards, containers, hula hoops, bean bags, glue, card, transparent containers, small objects, plates, cups, action cards (photocopiable 10), shells, precious stones

EXPLORE

Taking every opportunity throughout the school day to build and reinforce mathematical concepts gives children's learning purpose and meaning in the wider context of their lives.

ACTIVITY	AREA	DESCRIPTION	RESOURCES
Matching numerals	Maths area	Children match the digit cards 1–10 to transparent containers containing that number of objects.	Transparent containers, countable objects up to 10, digit cards 1–10
Counting bean bags	Hall or outside	Children roll the dice and then throw that number of bean bags into the hula hoop. They then count how many they actually got in the hoop.	Large dice, hula hoops, bean bags
Set the table	Home corner	Ask children to set the table ready for snack time for either 9 or 10 children.	Plates, cups

Unit 7: Numbers to 10, Week 3: Counting to 9 and 10

Day 1

Learning focus

Cardinality of 9 and 10

Before you teach

- How will you provide scaffolding to aid children to relate amounts of concrete materials to abstract numerals?
- How will you support children's counting throughout the day? Consider how counting can be incorporated into daily routines.
- How will you encourage children to count objects out from a larger group?

Starter

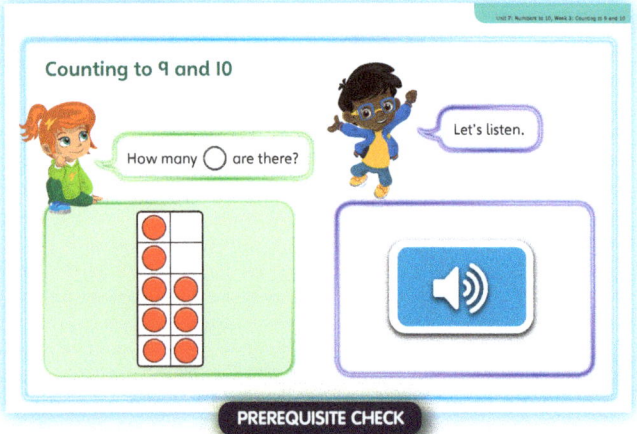

PREREQUISITE CHECK

PREREQUISITE CHECK Counting 8 counters shown in a ten frame.

WAYS OF WORKING Whole class

IN FOCUS The **Prerequisite check** confirms that children can count to 8 accurately when 8 is represented with counters on a ten frame. Some children may see that 8 can be made up of 5 and another 3.

ASK

- *What are these called?* [counters, ten frame]
- *Where will you start to count?*
- *How do you know when you have counted them all?*

STIMULUS Story: Birthday buttons

It was nearly Isha's birthday. Amna needed to find some buttons to decorate her friend's birthday card. Later that day, while tidying her bedroom and picking the socks up from under her bed, she felt a strange object. Amna pulled the object out from under the bed. It was a box. Amna shook the box and something inside rattled. Excited, Amna carefully opened the box and peered inside. There were … buttons! Lots of buttons, all different colours, shapes and sizes. 'Wow!' said Amna out loud. 'How many buttons are there?'

WAYS OF WORKING Whole class

Prepare a box containing a selection of 10 interesting buttons. Play the audio story and explain that you have brought Amna's box into class. Children can guess how many buttons there might be. Open the box and explain that you are going to count the buttons.

IN FOCUS When counting the buttons, focus on one-to-one correspondence, stable order and cardinality (the last number you say in a count being the total). Give each button to a child and line them up at the front of the class so you can count the buttons by pointing to each child. This will support the one-to-one correspondence of counting to 10, and will help children to avoid counting the items more than once.

ASK

- *How many buttons do you think there could be?*
- *Let's count them out one by one. How many buttons are there?*
- *Can you count them back into the box? Are there still the same number if you put them back in this order?*

GET ACTIVE Using the story as a stimulus, make button birthday cards. Children can choose up to 10 buttons to decorate their cards.

41

Day 2

Learning focus
Counting up to 10

Discover

WAYS OF WORKING Whole class or small groups
Ensure counters and ten frames are available to support children's learning. If possible, provide the items represented in the **Discover** picture so all children can physically count the objects.

IN FOCUS Children use one-to-one correspondence to count objects up to 10. They continue to develop their understanding of cardinality.

ASK
- How many containers are there in the picture?
- What different items can you see?
- Can you count the shells by pointing to each shell as you count?
- How can you use counters to help you count the shells? Can you use one counter for each shell?
- How might the ten frame help you to count the shells?

STRENGTHEN Have containers to represent those in the **Discover** picture. Use the actual objects (shells, badges, precious stones and buttons) if they are available, otherwise use cubes or counters to represent the objects. Count the objects out of the basket or jar by removing them one at a time.

DEEPEN Ask children to represent the **Discover** picture themselves by counting the relevant number of items into the container. Can they count them back out again?

Share

WAYS OF WORKING Whole class

IN FOCUS Children use a horizontal ten frame to support counting up to 10. Work to develop the understanding of filling the top row first to encourage children to develop the understanding of 9 and 10 as 5 and 4 more, or 5 and 5 more. Use the **Ten frame teaching tool** to replicate the ten frame in the **Share**.

ASK
- How many shells are there? Can you use the counters to represent the shells?
- How can you use a ten frame to count the shells? Can you fill the top row first and then move to the bottom row? There are 5 and 4 more, you have 9 altogether.
- Whose method do you like, Flo's or Astrid's? Can you say why you like their method?

STRENGTHEN Make a single line of counters on the floor. Show how you can move 4 counters to make a new line that looks like the ten frame arrangement. Encourage children to touch each counter as they count them and say the number of the last counter more loudly to reinforce cardinality.

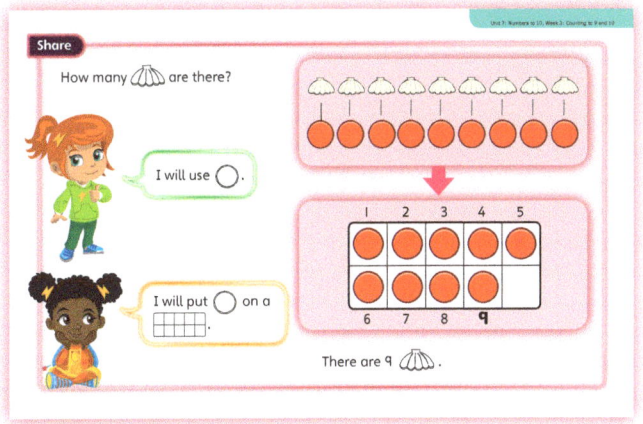

DEEPEN Draw children's attention to the numerals around the ten frame. Ask children if they can read them. Ask: *Can you represent each number using counters?*

GET ACTIVE Use ten frames and counters to count the other objects in the **Discover** picture. How many precious stones or badges are there? Ask children to make each number on a ten frame, encouraging them to fill the top row first.

Unit 7: Numbers to 10, Week 3: Counting to 9 and 10

Day 3

Learning focus
Counting different representations up to 10

Think together

WAYS OF WORKING Whole class
Ensure counters and ten frames are available to support children's learning.

IN FOCUS Children continue to count up to 10 by representing amounts using buttons and then counters on a ten frame. The ten frame is presented both vertically and horizontally. Draw children's attention to what Flo and Ash are saying and encourage them to use the words *same* and *different* to discuss the representations. Use the **Ten frame teaching tool** to replicate the questions and demonstrate how the ten frame can be rotated without the amount changing. As children become more confident, they should be able to recognise a number on a ten frame without counting. The small step of progression from Question ❶ to Question ❷ is the step from counting real objects (buttons) to counting mathematical representations of an amount (counters).

ASK
- *How many buttons or counters are there? Can you point to each one as you count? Can you start counting from 5 as you know there are 5 on the first row?*
- *How are the ten frames the same? Are there the same number of buttons and counters? Can you make both representations using ten frames and counters to check?*

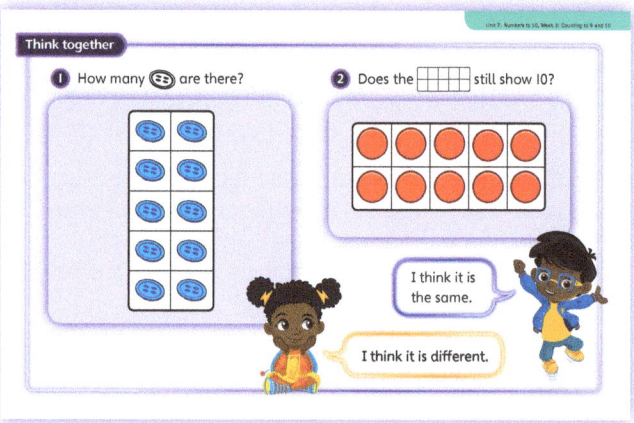

STRENGTHEN Count items out of a box by taking them out one at a time and placing them on ten frame. Fill the top row first followed by the bottom row.

DEEPEN Set up pictures of ten frames using the **Ten frame teaching tool** with the screen frozen so that you can just show it for a few seconds. Ask children to match the ten frame they see on screen by making it themselves. Ask: *How many counters are there altogether? Can you show the same amount in a different way on the ten frame?*

Practice: Journal 1

WAYS OF WORKING Independent thinking

IN FOCUS Children represent 9 and 10 in their own way on the ten frame. For the second part, children could draw round actual counters in the ten frame. Encourage children to touch each counter as they count. Some children may be able to write the numbers around the ten frame.

MASTERY CHECKPOINT Ensure that children have drawn the right number of flowers and counters on the ten frame. Check how children count the total: do they need to count one by one or are they beginning to subitise and use number bonds to make numbers more efficiently? Do they understand that 9 is one less than 10, so they have will have 2 full rows and then one less on the ten frame? Can they spot 9 and 10 without counting?

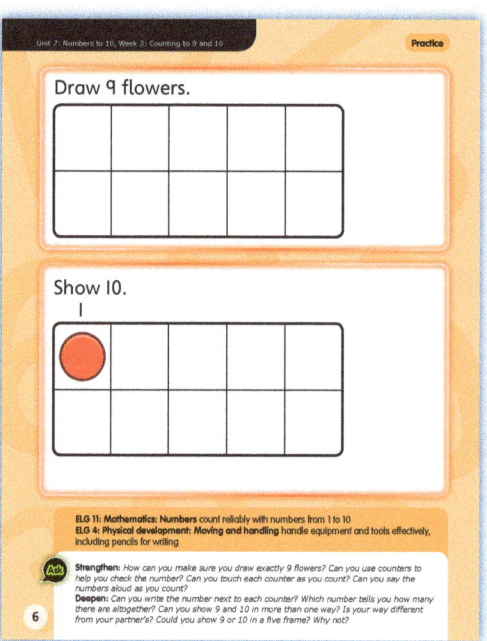

43

Unit 7: Numbers to 10, Week 3: Counting to 9 and 10

Day 4

Learning focus
Different representations of 9 and 10

Challenge

WAYS OF WORKING Whole class or pair work
Provide children with ten frames and counters to support learning. Encourage children who are confident to record the amount in each picture using numerals.

IN FOCUS Children will see different representations of 9 and 10, and will sort them into those that show 9 and those that show 10. Children make links between the representations and discuss what is the same and what is different about them.

ASK
- Which pictures show 9? Can you point to each item as you count? Can you make the pictures using real objects?
- Which picture shows the number 10?
- Do you need to count each object or can you see the number without counting?
- Which picture is the odd one out? Can you explain why it is the odd one out?

STRENGTHEN Model how to make the pictorial representations shown in the **Challenge**. Link each representation back to the ten frame and use it to check the number of items, for example, break up the cubes and place them on the ten frame to count how many, or model this using the **Ten frame teaching tool**.

DEEPEN Give children two large pieces of paper: one piece with the number 9 on it, one with the number 10 on it. Ask children to fill the paper with different representations of that number. They may use concrete and pictorial representations to make the number. Can any children write the numeral?

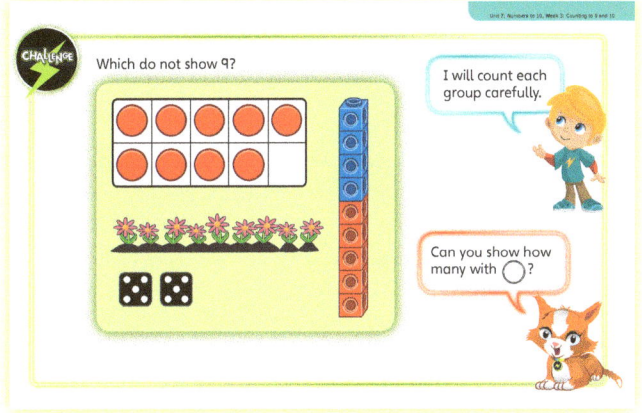

GET ACTIVE Label sets of two hoops with the numerals 9 and 10. Ask four pairs of children to make or draw the representations shown in the **Challenge** question and add them to the correct hoop. Ask two more children to show 9 and 10 in ten frames to add to the hoops. Ask the other children to collect groups of 9 or 10 items from around the classroom or outside area and put them in the relevant hoop.

Unit 7: Numbers to 10, Week 3: Counting to 9 and 10

Day 5

Learning focus
Count up to 10 from a larger group

Practical activities

WAYS OF WORKING Whole class
You will need digit cards 1–10 and action cards (photocopiable 10) for these activities.

IN FOCUS The focus of these activities is to encourage children to see that 9 and 10 can also be represented as an abstract amount. Children also count 9 or 10 from a larger amount. Encourage children to use containers to store the objects they count out and then to use a ten frame to double check they have counted correctly.

GET ACTIVE Card and action game
Use digit cards 1–10 and action cards showing star jumps, hopping, clapping and skipping.

Choose a digit card and an action card and ask children to do the action that many times.

Counting out from a larger group
Show children a large box containing about 30–40 items. Explain that lots of the items you have collected this week have been mixed together and you need to count them back out. Use the digit cards to choose a number and then ask children to count that number out from the larger group. Give each child a container to count the objects into. Once you have counted the objects out of the larger container, label how many items are in the smaller containers.

Reflect: Journal 2

WAYS OF WORKING Independent thinking
Have buttons and paper clips available for children to use to represent the **Reflect** activity.

IN FOCUS The focus of this activity is for children to count out 9 or 10 from a larger amount. Children consider different methods to help them count efficiently, including crossing out the items as they count, numbering the items as they count or putting counters on top of the items or on the ten frame. Children may need to use counters, lining them up to help them to count without missing any or counting any items more than once.

MASTERY CHECKPOINT **Children who have mastered this concept** can count to 10 using one-to-one correspondence. They can represent 9 and 10 on a ten frame. They are starting to recognise that they can count on using a ten frame understanding that a full row is 5. Children can count objects out from a larger group.

Children who have not yet mastered this concept can count objects in a straight line up to 10, touching each object as they count. They start to use the ten frame to support their counting but still need to count all the objects without making the link to counting on.

Children who have mastered this concept with greater depth can count to 10 efficiently and accurately. They are starting to subitise and can understand when they can count on to find the total without counting all the objects. Children can represent 9 and 10 in more than one way independently.

Unit 8
Comparing numbers within 10

Mastery Expert tip! *"When teaching this unit, I used the language* more *and* fewer *as often as possible in my classroom. We compared the number of children in different rows on the carpet and numbers of stickers on sticker charts to help children become more comfortable with this key language. It was great to hear the children using these words later on in our lesson!"*

Don't forget to watch the Comparing quantities video!

ELGs

This unit supports the following ELGs:

→ **ELG 11: Mathematics: Numbers**
count reliably with numbers from 1 to 20, place them in order and say which number is one more or one less than a given number

→ **ELG 12: Mathematics: Shape, space and measures**
use everyday language to talk about size, weight, capacity, position, distance, time and money to compare quantities and objects and to solve problems

→ **ELG 14: Understanding the world: The world**
know about similarities and differences in relation to places, objects, materials and living things

→ **ELG 4: Physical development: Moving and handling**
show good control and co-ordination in large and small movements
handle equipment and tools effectively, including pencils for writing

WHY THIS UNIT IS IMPORTANT

This unit focuses on practising the skill of comparing groups of objects up to 10, using the key mathematical vocabulary of *more*, *fewer*, *more than* and *less than*. Children are exposed to various misconceptions throughout the unit, including comparing groups where objects within each group are different sizes, shapes and colours. Towards the end of the unit, children are asked to represent 'more' or 'fewer' than a given number, leading into a discussion about 'finding the difference' between two numbers up to 10.

WAYS OF WORKING

After modelling how to compare groups by lining up objects, encourage children to work in pairs to make two groups and line them up next to each other. Use cubes and counters to represent objects in a group to support children with this physical representation of two groups.

WHERE THIS UNIT FITS

→ Unit 7: Numbers to 10
→ **Unit 8: Comparing numbers within 10**
→ Unit 9: Addition to 10

In this unit, children identify more or less than a number up to 10, introducing the concept of addition by combining two groups of objects and of subtraction as the difference between two amounts.

Link to Key Stage 1

Number – number and place value
- count to and across 100, forwards and backwards, beginning with 0 or 1, or from any given number; count, read and write numbers to 100 in numerals; count in multiples of twos, fives and tens
- identify and represent numbers using objects and pictorial representations including the number line, and use the language of: equal to, more than, less than (fewer), most, least
- given a number, identify one more and one less
- read and write numbers from 1 to 20 in numerals and words

Number – addition and subtraction
- represent and use number bonds and related subtraction facts within 20

The learning in this unit introduces the concepts of addition and subtraction pictorially by thinking about more or fewer when comparing two groups of objects.

Unit 8: Comparing numbers within 10

ASSESSING MASTERY

Children who have mastered this unit will be able to:
- use the words *more* and *fewer* to compare groups of up to 10 items
- start to find the difference between groups by counting on or counting back
- represent numbers to 10

COMMON MISCONCEPTIONS	STRENGTHENING UNDERSTANDING	GOING DEEPER
Children may think that if objects are larger, there are more of them.	Use a range of sizes of objects to compare, making sure that there are sometimes more and sometimes fewer of the larger object.	Show children objects that are not aligned properly so the larger objects take up more space or one line is more spread out. Challenge children to explain what is confusing about the layout and to correct it.
Children may think that when a line of objects is longer there must be more objects even when they are spread out more.	Use five frames, ten frames or number tracks to encourage children to spread objects out evenly when comparing them in lines.	Ask children to compare sets of 4–10 counters by placing them in two horizontal ten frames, filling the top row first. Can they explain how the ten frame shows which group has more or fewer without counting?

STRUCTURES AND REPRESENTATIONS

Ten frame: The ten frame helps to give children a sense of 10, and supports their understanding of number bonds to 10. It also plays a key role in helping children to compare two numbers.

Multilink cubes: Multilink cubes provide a physical representation of an amount, which children can use to count and compare.

Counters: Counters are used to represent objects being counted. They can be placed in the ten frame or lined up in a row.

RESOURCES

Mandatory: ten frame (photocopiable 6), multilink cubes, counters

Optional: building blocks (different sizes), plates, cups, toy animals or pictures of animals, soft toys, cushions, PE equipment (bibs, balls, bats), stickers, pencil pots, pencils, hula hoops, bean bags, number cards

TEACHING TOOLS

multilink cubes, ten frame

KEY LANGUAGE

There is some key language that children will need to know as part of the learning in this unit:
→ more, fewer/fewest
→ greater/greatest, smaller/smallest, large/largest, taller/tallest, shorter/shortest
→ compare, how many/**how many more**, different/difference

Unit 8: Comparing numbers within 10, Week 4: Comparing groups up to 10

Comparing groups up to 10

Learning focus
This week, children will compare numbers up to 10. They will focus on comparing groups of objects where the objects differ in size.

Small steps
→ Previous step: Counting to 9 and 10
→ **This step: Comparing groups up to 10**
→ Next step: Combining 2 groups to find the whole

COMMON MISCONCEPTIONS

Children may miscount the objects and so compare the groups inaccurately. Ask:
- *What could you use to help you count the objects?*
- *Can you line the objects up?*

Children may say that a greater number is smaller or vice versa. Ask:
- *What could you use to help you compare?*
- *Could you make the numbers using counters?*

Children may assume that larger objects represent a larger number. Ask:
- *How many objects are in this group? Which is more, 7 or 8? Which is fewer, 6 or 8?*

KEY LANGUAGE

In lesson: more, fewer, how many, different, **how many more**

Other language to be used by the teacher: greater, greatest, fewest, smaller, smallest, largest, taller, tallest, shorter, compare, difference

STRUCTURES AND REPRESENTATIONS

ten frame, multilink cubes

RESOURCES

Mandatory: ten frames, multilink cubes, counters

Optional: building blocks (different sizes), plates, cups, toy animals or pictures of animals, soft toys, cushions, PE equipment (bibs, balls, bats), stickers, pencil pots, pencils, hula hoops, bean bags, digit cards

EXPLORE

Taking every opportunity throughout the school day to build and reinforce mathematical concepts gives children's learning purpose and meaning in the wider context of their lives.

ACTIVITY	AREA	DESCRIPTION	RESOURCES
Tallest tower	Classroom	Challenge children to build the tallest tower possible using 5 blocks. This encourages children to understand that even though there is the same number of blocks, the tower may be a different height. Children consider how the height of the block affects the height of the tower.	Range of different sized building blocks
Setting the table	Snack area	Give children plates and cups (making sure there are not the same number of each) to set the table. Ask: *Are there more plates or cups? How many more?*	Plates, cups
Bean bags	Outside	Place some hula hoops around the outside area, each with a digit card inside or a card with a number represented in dots. Children identify the number and try to throw the same number of bean bags into each hoop. Take the digit cards out and let children choose how many bean bags to throw into each hoop and then choose the digit card to match each hoop. Discuss which hoops have more or fewer bean bags.	Hula hoops, bean bags, digit cards

Unit 8: Comparing numbers within 10, Week 4: Comparing groups up to 10

Day 1

Learning focus
Compare groups up to 10

Before you teach
- Are children confident counting forwards and backwards to and from 10?
- What resources and representations will you make available from previous lessons to support children's learning in this unit?

Starter

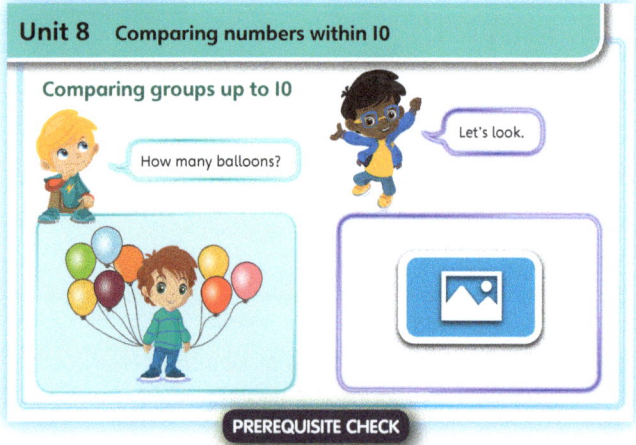

PREREQUISITE CHECK

PREREQUISITE CHECK Counting 8 balloons shown in two different-sized groups (5 and 3).

WAYS OF WORKING Whole class
Provide multilink cubes and a ten frame for children to represent groups of balloons.

IN FOCUS This **Prerequisite check** consolidates children's counting up to 8. The representations are presented in two unequal groups, one of 5 balloons and one of 3 balloons. Encourage children to count 5 balloons then count on the extra 3 to make 8 in total.

ASK
- Which balloons will you count first?
- Can you count on from 5 to find out how many balloons there are altogether?
- Which group shows more balloons? Does it matter that the balloons are different colours?

STIMULUS

STIMULUS Photograph prompting a guided activity

WAYS OF WORKING Whole class

IN FOCUS The **Stimulus** photograph of sheep and lambs will spark interest in the comparison activity. Encourage children to describe what they see, using the key vocabulary of *more* and *fewer*. Tease out descriptive language of comparison, asking children to describe the size and shapes of the animals.

ASK
- What can you see in the picture?
- Can you name the animals?
- How many of each animal are there?
- How many sheep and lambs are there altogether?

GET ACTIVE Encourage children to make a farmyard scene using toy animals (alternatively, you could use pre-printed photographs or pictures). Encourage children to compare the animals using the descriptive language of shape, colour and size. Count the different groups of animals and the numbers of animals in each group. Can children now compare the groups using numbers and the language of *more* and *fewer* as the comparison point?

Unit 8: Comparing numbers within 10, Week 4: Comparing groups up to 10

Day 2

Learning focus

Compare and represent numbers to 10

Discover

WAYS OF WORKING Whole class or small groups
Ensure toy animals or pictures of animals are available for children to use.

IN FOCUS The focus of the **Discover** is for children to compare representations of two amounts (hens and chicks) when there is variation in size, addressing the misconception that the larger representation (the hen) must always represent the biggest amount. Children also recap the core vocabulary of *more* and *fewer*.

ASK
- How many hens are there? How many chicks are there?
- Can you compare any other animals in the picture?
- Are there fewer sheep or fewer lambs?
- Why do 3 hens take up more space than 3 chicks? How can you compare them if they are different sizes? [By matching them up one-to-one.]

STRENGTHEN Use toy animals or pictures of the animals and line them up to help children count them more easily. This will also enable children to compare the number in each

group more effectively. They could place a counter or cube on each animal, then line them up to count them.

DEEPEN To extend thinking, ask: *Look at the hens and chicks. They take up the same amount of space, does that mean there are the same amount of each? How do you know?*

Share

WAYS OF WORKING Whole class

IN FOCUS Children use multilink cubes to represent the animals in the **Discover** picture, matching up the cubes to compare the groups of hens and chicks. Model matching up the cubes using the **Multilink cubes teaching tool**.

ASK
- How many hens are there? How many cubes do you need to show this?
- How many cubes do you need for the chicks?
- How does lining up the cubes help you to compare the groups?

STRENGTHEN If children are finding it difficult to use the cubes to represent the animals, use pictures of the actual animals (at the relative sizes) and line them up to compare them.

DEEPEN Ask children to look at the other animals in the **Discover** picture. Encourage children to compare these groups, prompting them to use the correct mathematical terminology of *more* and *fewer*. Can they draw their own comparison picture of two different groups of farmyard animals?

GET ACTIVE Ask children to get into teams of different sizes (4–10). Name each team, for example, 'team A', 'team B', and so on. Choose two teams, encouraging children to line themselves up to compare. Encourage the other children to make comparisons using prompt questions. Ask: *Which team has more children? Which team has fewer children? How many more are in team C than in team D?*

Unit 8: Comparing numbers within 10, Week 4: Comparing groups up to 10

Day 3

Learning focus

More than and fewer than

Think together

WAYS OF WORKING Whole class or small groups
View the **Online Flashcard** in single page mode to help children to focus on each question. Use the **Multilink cubes teaching tool** to model the comparison technique from **Share** and the **Ten frame teaching tool** to show how children can place counters on a ten frame for comparison. Provide cubes, counters and ten frames for children to use.

IN FOCUS Question ❶ follows on from the **Discover** and compares two groups of different sizes to find which has more. Question ❷ moves children's learning on a step by comparing fewer rather than more.

ASK
- Question ❶: *How many footballs are there? How many tennis balls are there?*
- Question ❶: *Can you use cubes or counters to represent the balls? Can you line them up to compare?*
- Question ❷: *How many bears are there altogether? How many cushions are there altogether?*
- Question ❷: *What does 'fewer' mean? Are there fewer cushions or fewer bears?*

STRENGTHEN Use bears and cushions from the classroom to recreate Question ❷. Put the items in two rows or sit the

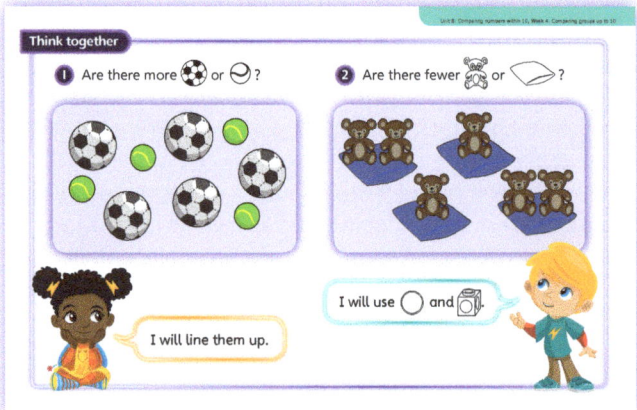

bears on top of the cushions to reinforce the matching of items in order to compare. Reinforce this learning by using different numbers of cushions and soft toys to check whether each toy can sit on a cushion. Keep returning to the language *more* and *fewer*.

DEEPEN Empty a bag of PE equipment containing bibs, balls and bats. Count out the balls and bibs together. Ask: *Are there more or fewer balls than bibs?* Ask children to wear the bibs and hold the balls to help them visualise if there are more or fewer balls compared to bibs. Repeat the activity with bats and bibs and with bats and balls.

Practice: Journal 1

WAYS OF WORKING Independent thinking

IN FOCUS The activities in the **Practice** encourage children to understand and use the language *more* and *fewer*. The objects differ in size to check children's understanding of whether size matters when comparing the number of objects. Extend thinking by asking if there are enough nests for all the birds in the first part and enough balloons for every teddy to have one each in the second part.

MASTERY CHECKPOINT Children who have mastered this activity can represent the objects with cubes and line them up to compare. They will use the language *more* and *fewer* correctly to describe the groups.

51

Unit 8: Comparing numbers within 10, Week 4: Comparing groups up to 10

Day 4

Learning focus

How many more?

Challenge

WAYS OF WORKING Whole class or in pairs
Ensure children know how to use cubes to represent the objects in the two groups and how to line them up to compare them. Practise with groups of two different objects if necessary and ask children to verbally compare the two groups using *more* and *fewer*. Use the **Ten frame teaching tool** to model how to organise the stickers in a way that makes the difference easier to see (5 circles along the top and 1 in the first space in the bottom row).

IN FOCUS In this **Challenge**, there are two variables for children to consider (shape and colour). Children now need to consider how many more of one type there are.

ASK
- Are all the stickers the same shape? How many stars are there? How many circles are there?
- What does the sticker chart look like? [A ten frame.] Can you make the groups with counters like Astrid?
- Have you lined them up? Can you see how many more circles there are? Can you count the circles that aren't lined up with a star?
- Does it matter that the stickers are different colours?

STRENGTHEN Use real stickers so children can make two lines to compare. Encourage them to draw lines between the rows of stickers to match them up and then count the extra stickers to find how many more or how many fewer. Children can place the stickers into two ten frames (circles in one, stars in another), filling up the top row first. Draw children's attention to the fact that because there are more than 5 circles, the top row is full and there is an extra one in the bottom row, making 6 altogether. There are fewer than 5 stars, so the top row is not full and there are no stars in the bottom row.

DEEPEN Ask: *How else could you compare the stickers? Could you look at colour?* Encourage children to use counters to compare the different colours of stickers and to describe how many more or how many fewer purple than silver.

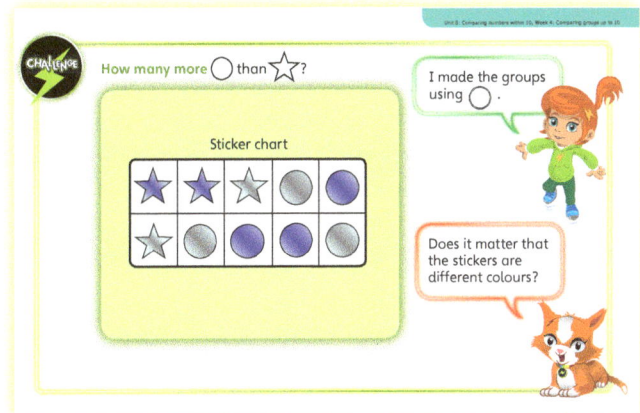

GET ACTIVE Allow children to use ten frames to make their own sticker charts. They should choose two shapes, each in two colourways, to fill the ten frame. With a partner they describe each other's chart using the terms *more* and *fewer* and saying how many more of one shape or colour there are.

Unit 8: Comparing numbers within 10, Week 4: Comparing groups up to 10

Day 5

Learning focus
Finding the difference

Practical activities

WAYS OF WORKING Whole class

IN FOCUS The focus of the **Practical activities** is to use the language of *more* and *fewer*, to encourage children to create groups that fit a rule given by the teacher and to find the difference between groups.

GET ACTIVE **Count and copy**
Explain that you are going to do an action for children to copy, but they need to listen and count the number of actions first before they copy your action. Demonstrate with an example: clap 5 times, counting each one. Say: *1, 2, 3, 4, 5. How many times did I clap? Can you clap more times than me?* Repeat the 5 claps. *Can you clap fewer times than me?* Repeat other actions 3–7 times (hopping, putting your hand up and down, tapping your head or nose), asking children to repeat it more or fewer times. Ask: *How many more times did you clap? How many fewer times did you clap?* Represent the number of actions with cubes or counters.

More or fewer items
Fill a pencil pot with 6 pencils. Ask: *What can you find that has more items in a pot? What can you find that has fewer items in a pot? Here is an empty pot, can you fill it with more pencils than I have? How many more pencils do you have? How can you check?* To give children opportunities to find the difference, ask them to work in pairs and each fill a pot with some pencils. Ask: *Which pot has more? What is the difference between the two pots (how many more pencils does the more pot have)?*

Reflect: Journal 2

WAYS OF WORKING Independent thinking

IN FOCUS Children use their understanding of more to draw more flowers than 5, and explain how many more they have drawn. Extend thinking by asking children **how many more** flowers they have drawn and, therefore, what the difference is between the original number of flowers and the number of flowers they have drawn.

MASTERY CHECKPOINT **Children who have mastered this concept** can use the words *more* and *fewer* to compare groups. They are starting to find the difference between groups.

Children who have not yet mastered this concept can identify which group has more or fewer by lining up the items. They are starting to use the language *more* and *fewer* independently.

Children who have mastered this concept with greater depth can use the words *more* and *fewer* to compare groups. They can compare groups and say how many more or fewer are in the groups by finding the difference.

53

Unit 9
Addition to 10

Mastery Expert tip! "Repeated practice of counting each part and recounting to find how many altogether helps children develop their understanding of the relationship between the two parts and the whole. It is important to use the vocabulary of *part* and *whole* throughout the week and make sure children can identify where these are on the models."

Don't forget to watch the Exploring composition video!

ELGs

This unit supports the following ELGs:

→ **ELG 11: Mathematics: Numbers**
count reliably with numbers from 1 to 20, place them in order and say which number is one more or one less than a given number
using quantities and objects, add and subtract 2 single-digit numbers and count on or back to find the answer

→ **ELG 14: Understanding the world: The world**
know about similarities and differences in relation to places, objects, materials and living things

WHY THIS UNIT IS IMPORTANT

This unit brings together the key skills of sorting from Unit 2, one more and one less from Unit 4 and the introduction to the part-whole model from Unit 6, to ensure confident mastery of the skill of combining two groups to find a whole up to 10. With addition of two groups, or parts, at its core, this unit brings together fundamental early learning concepts to provide a strong, structured basis from which to master addition to 10.

WAYS OF WORKING

Ensure that children have access to cubes and counters, each in two colours, for this unit, which they can use to represent the objects. Blank part-whole models will help children structure their work on parts and wholes and enable them to recreate the questions in the **Online Flashcards** and **Maths Journal**.

As gardening is the theme of this unit, plan to take learning outside where possible. The guided activity in the **Starter** is a stimulus for outside learning, and a great way to ensure children's understanding of two parts combining to make a whole is grounded in a real-life context.

WHERE THIS UNIT FITS

→ Unit 8: Comparing numbers within 10
→ **Unit 9: Addition to 10**
→ Unit 10: Number bonds to 10

In this unit, the part-whole model is used to introduce the concept of addition as the combining of two parts into a whole. The vocabulary of *altogether* is used throughout.

Link to Key Stage 1

Number – number and place value

- count to and across 100, forwards and backwards, beginning with 0 or 1, or from any given number; count, read and write numbers to 100 in numerals; count in multiples of twos, fives and tens
- identify and represent numbers using objects and pictorial representations including the number line, and use the language of: equal to, more than, less than (fewer), most, least
- given a number, identify one more and one less
- read and write numbers from 1 to 20 in numerals and words

Number – addition and subtraction

- represent and use number bonds and related subtraction facts within 20

The learning in this unit introduces the concept of addition shown pictorially as a part-whole model.

Unit 9: Addition to 10

ASSESSING MASTERY

Children who have mastered this unit will be able to:
- confidently use the vocabulary of *part* and *whole*
- accurately identify two parts and their combined whole
- add two parts to make a whole up to 10
- use a part-whole model to show two parts and the whole, in various orientations
- show that they understand that the two parts can be the same size
- understand which are the parts and which is the whole in a part-whole model
- show that they understand *altogether* as the combined total of all the parts

COMMON MISCONCEPTIONS	STRENGTHENING UNDERSTANDING	GOING DEEPER
Children may include the whole in their count when counting the parts in a part-whole model to find the whole.	Use different coloured counters for each part and provide plenty of practice moving the counters between the part and the whole to develop the understanding that the whole is a combination created by the two parts.	Give children sets of numbers or picture cards to put into or draw in a part-whole model. Ask: *Does it matter where the numbers go? Where does the largest number go?*
Children may think that the whole is always at the top. It is important to show the part-whole model in different orientations.	Use the **Part whole teaching tool** to show part-whole models in various orientations. Use blank part-whole models for children to create a part-whole model that can be turned around to show the whole in different places.	Children create a set of four part-whole models showing the same information but with the whole on the top, the left, the right and on the bottom.

STRUCTURES AND REPRESENTATIONS

Part-whole model: This model helps children understand that two or more things combine to make a whole.

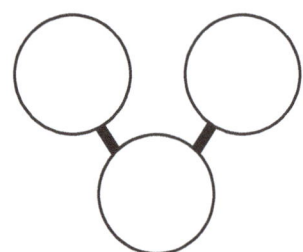

Counters: Using sets of differently coloured counters supports children's understanding of basic addition facts; that two or more amounts can be combined to make a whole.

Multilink cubes: Multilink cubes are excellent for demonstrating number and size relationships and to count and compare.

RESOURCES

Mandatory: hula hoops, pots, soil, seedlings, counters, multilink cubes, part-whole models (photocopiable 7)

Optional: flowers, pipe-cleaner flowers or pictures of flowers, tissue paper, similar objects for sorting (coloured balls, different sized bricks, coloured toy cars), sets of items for sorting (apples and bananas on plates, thin brushes and thick brushes in paint pots, piles of large and small stones, toy cows and horses), digit cards

TEACHING TOOLS

part whole

KEY LANGUAGE

There is some key language that children will need to know as part of the learning in this unit:
- count, part, whole,
- **altogether**, how many, total
- 1, 2, 3, 4, 5, 6, 7, 8, 9, 10
- addition, adding together, counting
- more, fewer

Unit 9: Addition to 10, Week 5: Combining 2 groups to find the whole

Combining 2 groups to find the whole

Learning focus
This week, children will develop confidence in using the part-whole model, being able to identify the whole and the parts in different orientations and understanding that the combined parts make the whole. The key vocabulary *altogether* is introduced as a term to describe the combined parts.

Small steps
→ Previous step: Comparing groups up to 10
→ **This step: Combining 2 groups to find the whole**
→ Next step: Using a ten frame

COMMON MISCONCEPTIONS
When counting the parts in a part-whole model to find the whole, children may include the whole in their count. Encourage children to count out loud, using concrete objects such as cubes or counters to represent the whole and parts. Ask:
- *Where is the whole on this model? Where are the parts? How many parts make this whole? Do you need to count the whole as well?*

Children may think that the whole is always at the top. It is important to show the part-whole model in different orientations. Ask:
- *Where is the whole? Where are the parts? Does the whole always need to be at the top?*
- *Can you make a part-whole model with the whole at the bottom? Can you make a part-whole model with the whole at the side?*

KEY LANGUAGE
In lesson: count, part, whole, **altogether**, how many, 1, 2, 3, 4, 5, 6, 7, 8, 9, 10

Other language to be used by the teacher: total, addition, adding together, more, fewer

STRUCTURES AND REPRESENTATIONS
part-whole model, cubes, counters

RESOURCES
Mandatory: hula hoops, pots, soil, seedlings, counters, multilink cubes, part-whole model (photocopiable 7)

Optional: flowers, pipe-cleaner flowers or pictures of flowers, tissue paper, similar objects for sorting (coloured balls, different sized bricks, coloured toy cars), sets of items for sorting (apples and bananas on plates, thin brushes and thick brushes in paint pots, piles of large and small stones, toy cows and horses), digit cards

EXPLORE
Taking every opportunity throughout the school day to build and reinforce mathematical concepts gives children's learning purpose and meaning in the wider context of their lives.

ACTIVITY	AREA	DESCRIPTION	RESOURCES
Hoops	Outside	Tape hula hoops to the floor in the shape of a part-whole model. Encourage children to use the hoops to create their own number stories. Provide a variety of objects and ask children to sort them into the hoops. Ask: *What are the parts? What is the whole? How many have you got altogether?*	Similar objects for sorting (red balls and blue balls, large bricks and small bricks, red cars and blue cars), hula hoops
Sorting and counting	Classroom	Provide a variety of sets of items for children to sort into two parts. They count parts and recount to find how many altogether.	Sets of items for sorting (apples and bananas on plates, thin brushes and thick brushes in paint pots, piles of large and small stones, toy cows and horses)
How many cubes?	Classroom	In pairs, children each take a small handful of cubes and count them. They compare and combine with their partner. Ask: *Who has the most? How many do you have altogether?*	Multilink cubes

Unit 9: Addition to 10, Week 5: Combining 2 groups to find the whole

Day 1

Learning focus

Recapping the language of parts and wholes

Before you teach

- Can children count a group of objects accurately?
- Can children identify similarities and differences between two groups of the same type of objects?
- Can children identify the parts and the whole on a part-whole model?

Starter

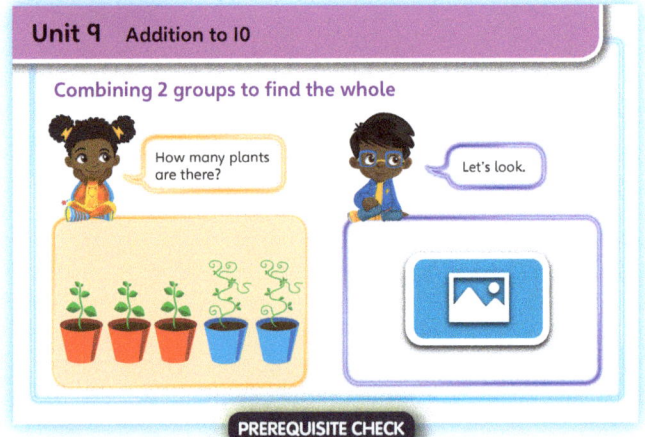

PREREQUISITE CHECK

PREREQUISITE CHECK Counting pots of seedlings shown in two distinct groups.

WAYS OF WORKING Whole class

IN FOCUS Discuss what children can see in the picture. Do children count the red pots and blue pots separately? How do they count the total number of plants? This provides a real-life context for combining two groups to count how many altogether.

ASK

- *Can you count the plants in the red pots? How many plants are in blue pots?*
- *Are there more or fewer red pots than blue pots?*
- *What is different about the plants?* [Colour of pot, shape of plant.]

STIMULUS

STIMULUS Photograph prompting a guided activity

WAYS OF WORKING Whole class

Ask children what they can see in the photograph. Have they seen any of these before? The photograph shows children planting seedlings. Explain that they are going to do some planting. Show two different types of seedlings or plants. How many of each type can they see? How many plants will they plant altogether?

IN FOCUS The **Stimulus** provides a real-life context for combining two groups to count how many altogether. Moving the plants to one side or touching each plant as they count them will help support one-to-one correspondence. Children need to understand that they can count to see how many in each part and then recount to find the total amount in the group. Some children may be able to start the count with the number in the first set, for example: 3 ... 4, 5 altogether.

ASK

- *How many of each type of plant are there?*
- *How many plants are there altogether?*

GET ACTIVE Provide pots, soil or compost and two distinct types of seedlings for children to plant 2–5 of each seedling. Encourage them to count how many of each seedling there are and how many seedlings they have planted altogether. You could also use plastic flowers of two distinct colours or shapes to model planting.

Unit 9: Addition to 10, Week 5: Combining 2 groups to find the whole

Day 2

Learning focus
Combining two parts to make a whole

Discover

WAYS OF WORKING Whole class

Have real flowers or pipe cleaner flowers of two different types available so that children can physically count each part and then recount to see how many make the whole group of flowers.

IN FOCUS The **Discover** flashcard provides a real life context for combining two parts to make a whole: Amna has some red tulips and some yellow daffodils to plant in her pot. How many flowers will she plant altogether? Children should also be encouraged to discuss what other parts and wholes they can see in the picture, reinforcing the concept that two parts can be combined to make a whole group.

ASK
- Can you say what 'altogether' means?
- How many red tulips are there? How many yellow daffodils? How many flowers altogether?
- What else can you see in the picture? What are the parts and wholes?

STRENGTHEN Allow children to use pictures, cubes or counters to represent the different parts and to count them all or draw them in the whole on a blank part-whole model

to see how many altogether. They should be encouraged to tell the number story as they add the objects: *There are 2 big clouds and 3 small clouds. There are 5 clouds altogether.* Use stem sentences as a structure: ___ is a part and ___ is a part. ___ is the whole. Altogether there are ___.

DEEPEN Encourage children to describe other parts and wholes they can see in the **Discover**. Can children guess what their partner is looking at from the clues they give? For example: *I can see a part of 3 and a part of 5. What am I looking at? I can see a whole group of 5. What am I looking at?*

Share

WAYS OF WORKING Whole class

IN FOCUS The focus of **Share** is to ensure that children are aware that the whole represents the two parts combined. Use single page view to first show the picture from **Discover**, and move to full view to show how this translates to the part-whole model with the parts (red flowers and yellow flowers) moving into the whole to show how many there are altogether. Model moving the parts into the whole using the flowers on the **Part whole teaching tool**. Ensure children are confident with representing objects using counters. The **Part whole teaching tool** can be used to show the process using counters. Use the option to show the number of objects to introduce children to the abstract representation using numerals.

ASK
- Which are the parts? Which is the whole?
- How many are in each part? How many are in the whole?

STRENGTHEN Moving pipe cleaner flowers or pictures of flowers back and forth between the parts and the whole will help to develop a secure understanding of this relationship. Prompt children to tell the number story: *There are 3 red flowers and 4 yellow flowers. There are 7 flowers altogether.*

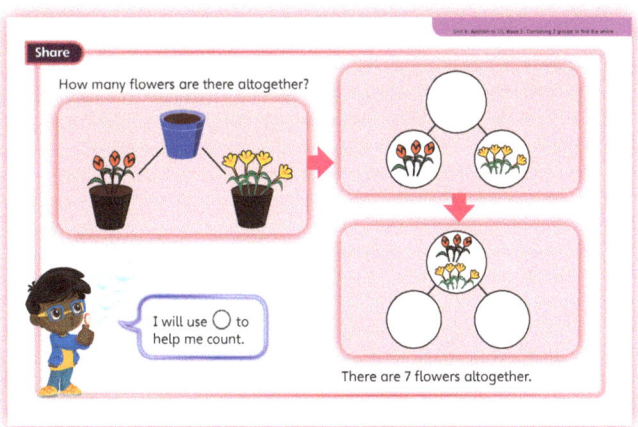

DEEPEN Encourage children to create a part-whole model to represent something else they can see in the picture. Ask: *Can you make a part-whole model for the clouds? What are the parts representing? What is the whole representing?* Encourage children to tell the number story.

GET ACTIVE Using small hoops, ask children to choose some items to put into the parts and then find the whole (ensuring the whole equals the total of the two parts). Children replace the items with counters, then with digit cards.

Unit 9: Addition to 10, Week 5: Combining 2 groups to find the whole

Day 3

Learning focus
Identifying the whole

Think together

WAYS OF WORKING Whole class
Encourage children to use concrete manipulatives to represent the objects and move them between the parts and whole. Ask children to count each part and then recount to find the whole group. Encourage them to create a number story as they play. Use the **Part whole teaching tool** to show a part-whole model in various orientations, drawing out that this does not affect the total.

IN FOCUS Question ❶ builds on **Share** and children see that sometimes the parts can be the same. This will be explored further when children are introduced to doubling in Unit 15. Continue to reinforce the language of *whole* and *parts*. In Question ❷, the part-whole model is shown in a different orientation for the first time. Ensure that children understand which is the whole and which are the parts.

ASK
- Question ❶: *How many flowers can you see in each part? How many flowers are there altogether? Can you see without counting each flower?*
- Question ❷: *What do you notice about the part-whole model this time? Is Flo right? Where is the whole now? Where are the parts? Does it matter that the whole is in a different position? How can you tell which is the whole? How many butterflies are in each part? How many altogether?*

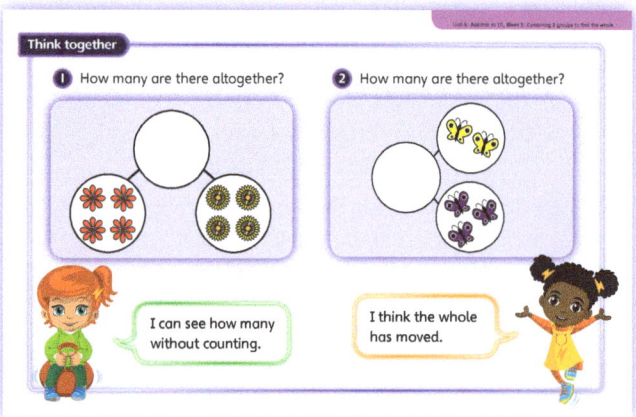

STRENGTHEN Ask children to place pipe cleaner flowers, pictures of flowers or cubes into the two parts of a blank part-whole model. Count the flowers into the whole and back into the parts. Rotate the model so that the whole is on the side. Ask: *Where are the two parts now? Where is the whole? Does the whole stay the same, even if you move it? How do you know?* Demonstrate this using the **Part whole teaching tool**.

DEEPEN Take every opportunity to explore the part-whole model in various orientations. Ask: *Is it possible to have the whole at the bottom of the part-whole model?* Move concrete objects between the parts and the whole. Encourage children to tell a number story about the part-whole model they create.

Practice: Journal 1

WAYS OF WORKING Independent thinking

IN FOCUS The focus of this **Practice** is to reinforce the vocabulary of *parts* and *whole* and to embed the understanding that the two parts are combined to make the whole group and recounted to see how many altogether. The part-whole model is shown in two different orientations.

MASTERY CHECKPOINT Children who have mastered this concept can say how many are in each part and how many there are altogether in the whole. They can show this using concrete resources on a part-whole model or by drawing in their journals. They can use a part-whole model to tell a number story.

Day 4

Learning focus
Exploring misconceptions using the part-whole model

Challenge

WAYS OF WORKING Whole class or in pairs
Children can use concrete resources to help them to identify which are the parts and which is the whole. Stem sentences can be used to support their reasoning. ___ is a part. ___ is a part. ___ is the whole. There are ___ altogether.

IN FOCUS The focus of this **Challenge** is for children to become secure in identifying the whole and the parts and comfortable with the part-whole model. As this may be the first time they have seen the parts and the whole represented at the same time, they may count all three amounts to find how many altogether. The whole is also shown at the bottom for the first time. Children should be encouraged to discuss and explain why each character thinks that their answer is the whole. This will deepen their understanding of the common misconceptions that occur when using the part-whole model.

ASK
- What do you think are the parts? Where is the whole?
- Why does Astrid think that 4 is the whole?
- Why does Dexter think that 10 is the whole?
- What do you think the whole is?

STRENGTHEN Some children may need to practise combining a variety of small objects practically before coming back to this **Challenge**. Use the Hoops activity from **Explore** to allow children to place items in the parts and replicate them in the whole. Encourage children to walk around the part-whole model made from hoops so that they can see it from different orientations, pointing out where the whole is each time.

DEEPEN Deepen thinking by asking children what advice they would give to Astrid and Dexter to help them to interpret the part-whole model. Prompt thinking by asking: *Can you draw a picture to help them understand?* Using the **Part whole teaching tool** or a blank part-whole model, show an incorrect part-whole model, where the whole is not the total of the parts. Encourage children to spot the mistake and correct it.

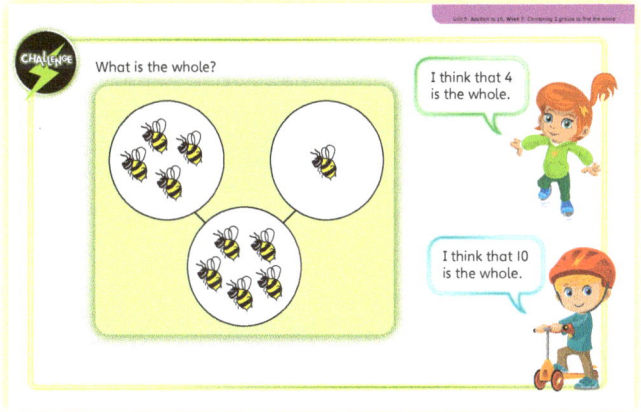

GET ACTIVE Create a role-play garden centre and encourage children to make flowers using pipe cleaners. They use the flowers and plant pots to explore part-whole models, partitioning and recombining to make the parts and the whole. Encourage them to tell the number story as they move the flowers. Stem sentences can be used to provide structure for these: *There are ___ and ___. There are ___ altogether.*

Unit 9: Addition to 10, Week 5: Combining 2 groups to find the whole

Day 5

Learning focus
Number stories using the part-whole model to 10

Practical activities

WAYS OF WORKING Whole class and small groups

IN FOCUS These **Practical activities** will consolidate children's understanding that two parts can be counted together to find the total or the whole. Children should stand in a circle so that everyone can see and move about. The first activity also helps children to see that two parts and a whole do not need to be physical objects that they can see and touch, but can be abstract, for example, movements and sounds.

GET ACTIVE **Count the claps**
Ask children to listen or watch carefully. Clap twice and then clap three times. Ask: *How many claps altogether?* Next, hop once on one foot and three times on the other. Ask: *How many hops altogether?* Repeat this game using jumps, clicks, nods, dropping counters into a tin, tapping your head and so on. Can children copy your actions? Split children into small groups and ask them to repeat the activity, each taking turns to clap, hop or nod. Ask each group to perform in turn at the front of the class. Ask the rest of the class: *How many claps/hops/nods were in each part? How many altogether?*

Hoops
Place three hoops on the floor to represent a part-whole model. Use tape to show the connecting lines. Ask 3 children to stand in one part and 1 child to stand in another. Together, count each part, and then ask all children in the parts to move into the whole and count them again. Replace children with objects, and encourage children to walk around the large part-whole model so that they see it in different orientations. Repeat with different numbers of children in each hoop.

Reflect: Journal 2

WAYS OF WORKING Independent thinking
There should be a selection of practical equipment available for children to use to represent the objects in their number stories, including cubes and counters in two different colours.

IN FOCUS The focus of this **Reflect** is to allow children to create their own part-whole model. This could be linked to a story that you have read, or children could make up their own story. Look out for children who might start putting too many objects into each part so that they are unable to count them accurately, so limit to 10 items in total. Children can place concrete resources on the model before drawing it in their journal.

MASTERY CHECKPOINT **Children who have mastered this concept** can use the language of *part* and *whole*. They can count how many in each part and recount to find how many altogether in the whole group.

Children who have not yet mastered this concept need support and prompts to confidently identify parts and wholes and may also need support with number bonds to 10.

Children who have mastered this concept with greater depth can use part-whole models in different orientations, explaining which is the whole and which are the parts. They can identify errors and explain why they have happened.

61

Unit 10
Number bonds to 10

Mastery Expert tip! "Asking children to show the bonds to 10 in different representations, including on their fingers, and encouraging them to describe what they could see really helped them to embed these key facts and to understand commutativity."

Don't forget to watch the Exploring composition video!

ELGs

This unit supports the following ELGs:

→ **ELG 11: Mathematics: Numbers**
count reliably with numbers from 1 to 20, place them in order and say which number is one more or one less than a given number
using quantities and objects, add and subtract 2 single-digit numbers and count on or back to find the answer

→ **ELG 4: Physical development: Moving and handling**
show good control and co-ordination in large and small movements
handle equipment and tools effectively, including pencils for writing

WHY THIS UNIT IS IMPORTANT

This unit explores the vital building block for understanding number, the bonds to 10. These are represented in a ten frame and in part-whole models and using counters. The learning in this unit forms the basis for understanding addition (including the commutative law), which can then be applied to larger numbers. Key language related to both addition and subtraction is used throughout.

WAYS OF WORKING

Ensure that children have access to double-sided counters (or counters in two colours) for this unit, which they can use to represent the objects. Blank ten frames and part-whole models will help children structure their work and enable them to recreate the questions in the **Online Flashcards** and **Maths Journal**.

WHERE THIS UNIT FITS

→ Unit 9: Addition to 10
→ **Unit 10: Number bonds to 10**
→ Unit 13: Counting on and counting back

In this unit, children continue exploring addition, now looking specifically at the number bonds to 10. These are shown in a ten frame and using the whole-part model, which have both been used before. Children begin to explore the bonds in a more systematic way and recognise the commutative law of addition. Children are introduced to missing parts as a precursor to subtraction by counting on or back.

Link to Key Stage 1

Number – number and place value

- count to and across 100, forwards and backwards, beginning with 0 or 1, or from any given number; count, read and write numbers to 100 in numerals; count in multiples of twos, fives and tens
- identify and represent numbers using objects and pictorial representations including the number line, and use the language of: equal to, more than, less than (fewer), most, least
- given a number, identify one more and one less
- read and write numbers from 1 to 20 in numerals and words.

Number – addition and subtraction

- represent and use number bonds and related subtraction facts within 20

A solid understanding of the number bonds to 10 is the foundation of understanding all number bonds.

Unit 10: Number bonds to 10

ASSESSING MASTERY

Children who have mastered this unit will be able to:
- confidently use the vocabulary of number bonds and addition
- accurately identify pairs of numbers with a total of 10
- use a ten frame and a part-whole model to represent bonds to 10
- understand that if 8 and 2, for example, make 10, then so must 2 and 8

COMMON MISCONCEPTIONS	STRENGTHENING UNDERSTANDING	GOING DEEPER
Children may not see that the whole is the sum of the parts in a part-whole model.	Using counters, encourage children to lay out the amount in each part in a long line or in the ten frame format to compare the sum of the two parts with the total in the whole.	Ask children to identify the whole, given the two parts, or the missing part given the whole and one part.
Children may use a random approach to finding number bonds to 10, missing some of them.	Use a bead string, starting with 5 and 5 and moving one bead at a time to show 6 and 4, 7 and 3 and so on.	Ask children to show the pattern of the bonds to 10, starting with 10 and 0, 9 and 1.
Children may not be aware of the commutative law of addition, seeing 8 and 2 as a separate number bond from 2 and 8.	Use paper plates to show the part-whole model and switch the parts around. Display number bonds on the **Ten frame teaching tool** and rotate.	Can children say or show the related bond, given one, such as 7 and 3? Can children prove that 3 and 7 is the same as 7 and 3?

STRUCTURES AND REPRESENTATIONS

Ten frame: Ten frames help children to visualise bonds to 10.

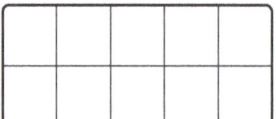

Part-whole model: Part-whole models offer an alternative way of visualising bonds to 10, understanding that pairs of numbers combine to make a total of 10.

Counters: Counters can be placed in the ten frame or lined up in a row. Use two different colours for each part of the bond.

Bead string: Bead strings are a great way of introducing patterns and missing numbers and helping children be systematic in their approach. They can represent numbers and split numbers into parts, and show the effect of adding two numbers together.

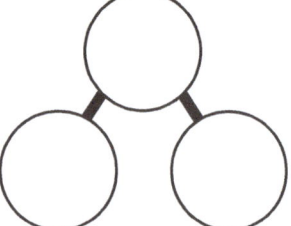

RESOURCES

Mandatory: double-sided counters or counters in two colours, drinking bottles, ten frames (photocopiable 6), blank part-whole model (photocopiable 7), multilink cubes

Optional: bead strings, 0–10 digit cards, 10 plastic bottles or skittles, soft ball, playdough, cake candles (sets of 10 in at least two colours), buttons, paper plates, glue, paper shapes, hula hoops, bean bags, ladybird template (photocopiable 9), small part-whole models (photocopiable 11), toy fish, bowls, large play bricks

TEACHING TOOLS

part whole, ten frame

KEY LANGUAGE

There is some key language that children will need to know as part of the learning in this unit:
- group, count, counters, 1, 2, 3, 4, 5, 6, 7, 8, 9, 10
- how many altogether, how many more, how many fewer, more than, fewer than, less than, each
- ten frame, part-whole model, whole, part, bead string
- missing number, one more, one less, add, number bond to 10

Unit 10: Number bonds to 10, Week 6: Using a ten frame

Using a ten frame

Learning focus

This week, children will explore number bonds to 10 using a variety of representations. Children will progress from seeing concrete representations to pictorial representations (counters), finally using counters on a ten frame to show all number bonds to 10. They will answer 'how many altogether' and 'how many more' questions.

Small steps

→ Previous step: Combining two groups to find the whole
→ **This step: Using a ten frame**
→ Next step: The part-whole model to 10

COMMON MISCONCEPTIONS

Children may not be aware that 8 and 2 is equivalent to 2 and 8 (the commutative law of addition), so may see these as separate number bonds. Ask:
- *How many do you have here? What happens if you swap the groups around? Is the total the same or different?*

Children may find it difficult to identify what is missing. They may instead count what is there. Encourage children to use ten frames to help them to count the missing objects, using counters in a different colour to represent what is missing. Ask:
- *How many are hidden or missing? How is it possible to count things that are not there?*

KEY LANGUAGE

In lesson: group, count, how many altogether, how many more, ten frame, counters, 1, 2, 3, 4, 5, 6, 7, 8, 9, 10

Other language to be used by the teacher: missing number, more than, fewer than, less than, number bond to 10

STRUCTURES AND REPRESENTATIONS

ten frame, counters

RESOURCES

Mandatory: double-sided counters or counters in two colours, drinking bottles, ten frames

Optional: bead strings, 1–10 digit cards, 10 plastic bottles or skittles, soft ball, playdough, cake candles (sets of 10 in at least two colours), ladybird template (photocopiable 9), large play bricks

EXPLORE

Taking every opportunity throughout the school day to build and reinforce mathematical concepts gives children's learning purpose and meaning in the wider context of their lives.

ACTIVITY	AREA	DESCRIPTION	RESOURCES
Spots on the ladybird	Classroom	Provide large laminated ladybirds and counters in two colours. Ask children to use the counters to put 10 spots on the ladybirds. How many ways can they find to do this?	Laminated ladybird template (photocopiable 9), counters in two colours
Skittles	Outside	Arrange the 10 bottles like skittles. Children take turns to roll a ball to knock them down. They should choose how to record the number of skittles standing and fallen using pictures, numerals or other representations.	10 plastic bottles or skittles, soft ball
How many am I hiding?	Classroom	Show children a bead string with 10 beads. Establish that there are exactly 10 beads. Cover some with your hand and show children the remaining beads. Children use various strategies to find the hidden number. They could then play independently in pairs or small groups.	10 bead string
Birthday cupcakes	Art area	Children work in small groups to decorate a playdough cake with 10 candles to represent a number bond to 10. Each group has 20 candles, 10 in one colour, 10 in a different colour. Ask: *How many different ways can you show 10?*	Playdough, candles (sets of 10 in at least two colours)

Unit 10: Number bonds to 10, Week 6: Using a ten frame

Day 1

Learning focus
Exploring the composition of 10

Before you teach
- Can children count up to 10 objects?
- Do children understand that numbers can be partitioned into pairs or groups of smaller numbers?
- Are children secure with their number bonds to 5?

Starter

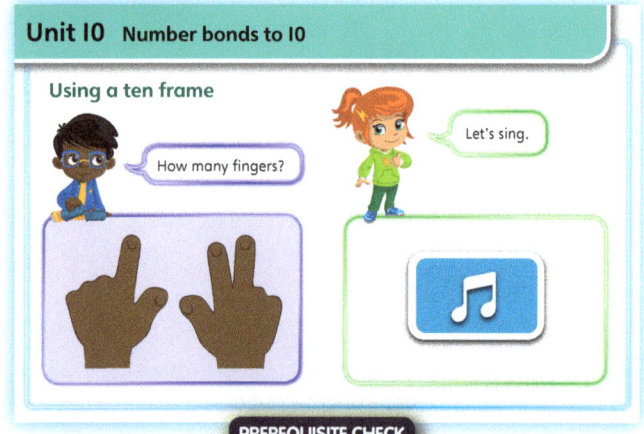

PREREQUISITE CHECK

PREREQUISITE CHECK Picture of a pair of hands holding up 2 and 3 fingers.

WAYS OF WORKING Whole class and pairs
Introduce this unit's first week of teaching with the **Prerequisite check**. Encourage children to show the same amounts using their own fingers to support their understanding. Ask: *How else can you show 5 with both hands?*

IN FOCUS Using knowledge of number bonds to 5, children should answer the question, *How many fingers?* They should also consider other ways of showing 5 using the fingers on both hands. Encourage children to say what their fingers are showing: *2 and 3 make 5 altogether*. In pairs, one child shows up to 4 fingers and their partner shows the number of fingers to make 5 in total.

ASK
- *How many fingers can you see on this hand?*
- *How many fingers can you see on both hands altogether?*
- *Can you show 5 using different fingers from those in the picture?*

10 green bottles
10 green bottles standing on the wall,
10 green bottles standing on the wall,
And if one green bottle should accidentally fall,
There'll be 1 on the floor and 9 left on the wall.
[Repeat this through 9, 8, 7, 6, 5, 4, 3, 2, …]
1 green bottle standing on the wall,
1 green bottle standing on the wall,
And if that one bottle should accidentally fall,
There'll be 10 on the floor and none left on the wall.

STIMULUS

STIMULUS Song: 10 green bottles

WAYS OF WORKING Whole class

IN FOCUS The song in the **Stimulus** introduces children to the idea that 10 can be made up of different pairs of numbers, which could be recorded by the teacher as they sing the song. The song will provide a context for finding number bonds to 10, as the standing and fallen bottles will always equal 10. Encourage children to count the number of bottles standing and fallen after each verse and to count all of the bottles to understand that there are still 10 in total.

ASK
- *How many bottles are standing on the wall?*
- *How many bottles have fallen?*
- *How many bottles are there altogether?*
- *If one more bottle falls, how many will still be standing?*
- *Will there always be 10 bottles altogether, even though some of them have fallen over? How do you know?*

GET ACTIVE As you sing the song together, encourage children to represent the bottles with their fingers and to fold a finger down when the bottle falls in each verse. Alternatively, sing the song again, giving space between each verse for children to show what is happening with counters. Give pairs of children 10 counters to represent the bottles. They put the counters in a horizontal row and count them to make sure they have exactly 10. As the class sings the song again, a verse at a time, they move one counter down. Encourage children to start at either end, rather than moving random counters down, so removing counter 10, then 9 and so on, or counter 1 then counter 2.

Unit 10: Number bonds to 10, Week 6: Using a ten frame

Day 2

Learning focus

Exploring the composition of 10, moving from concrete to pictorial representations

Discover

WAYS OF WORKING Whole class or small groups

IN FOCUS The focus of **Discover** is to show children a clear representation of 10 using concrete objects in a familiar context. Building on knowledge of combining two parts to make a whole from Unit 9, children can see that there are 10 bottles altogether, even though some have fallen over.

ASK
- How many bottles are standing?
- How many are on the floor?
- How many bottles are there altogether?

STRENGTHEN Replay the **Stimulus** song from the **Starter** and encourage children to sing along. Collect 10 empty drinking bottles and encourage children to line up the 10 bottles and lay one down after each verse of the song. What do they notice? Build a wall outside with large play bricks and stand 10 bottles on it to mimic the song. Ask a child to take one bottle off as you sing each verse, laying it on the floor under where it stood, as in the **Discover** picture. Repeat the bonds shown together, for example: *8 and 2 is 10.*

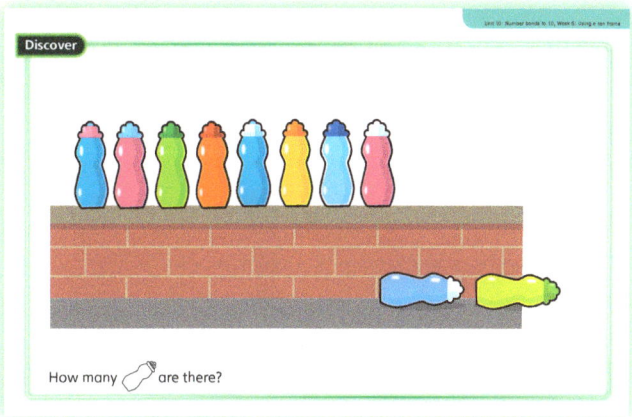

DEEPEN Extend thinking by asking children about all possible number bonds to 10. What if 7 bottles are standing and 3 have fallen down, are there still 10 in total? What if 6 bottles are standing and 4 have fallen down? Do children notice anything about the pairs of numbers you are using? Use drinking bottles to demonstrate these number bonds.

Share

WAYS OF WORKING Whole class

Ensure empty drinking bottles, double-sided counters or counters in two colours and ten frames are available for children to replicate the counting methods demonstrated in **Share**. Use single page view to focus on one step at a time. Ask children to say the answer sentence together, *8 and 2 is 10*, as this will help to reinforce the number bond. The **Ten frame teaching tool** can be used to model the **Share** and rotated to demonstrate commutativity.

IN FOCUS The focus of **Share** is to model two steps for answering the **Discover** question: counting the two groups and representing them with counters, then placing the counters on a ten frame to structure the count.

ASK
- What has Dexter done to help him count all the bottles?
- What do the red counters show? What do the yellow counters show?
- What is Flo using to help her count?
- Does it matter that the counters are different colours?
- Can you see how many counters there are in the ten frame, without counting each one? How many counters are in the top row? How many in the bottom row? How many altogether?

STRENGTHEN Encourage children to play with ten frames and to change the amount of red and yellow counters

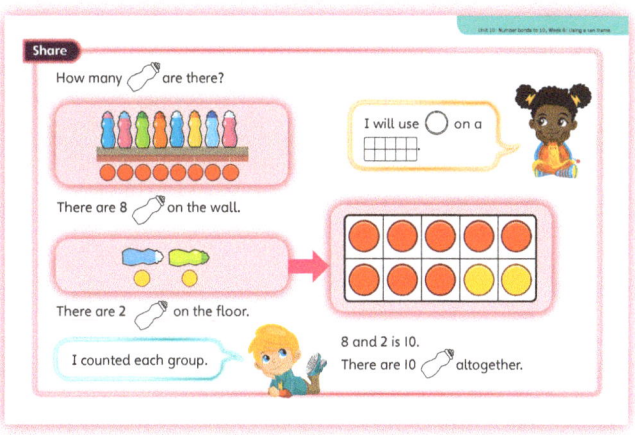

themselves, while ensuring that the frame is always full, with one counter in each space. Can they draw the different representations they make?

DEEPEN Ask children to work with a partner to find all the various ways of showing 10 on the ten frame using two colours of counters. Start them off with 5 counters of each colour, and demonstrate the first couple of number bonds to get them started. Discuss commutativity with children, for example that 4 and 6 is the same as 6 and 4. Both total 10. Demonstrate using the counters and swapping the colours.

Unit 10: Number bonds to 10, Week 6: Using a ten frame

Day 3

Learning focus

Exploring the composition of 10 by reinforcing different representations of 10

Think together

WAYS OF WORKING Whole class
Ensure that two colours of counters and blank ten frames are available.

IN FOCUS The focus of **Think together** is to practise the method of working out how many altogether by first identifying how many bottles are on the wall and then looking at how many are on the floor. Astrid prompts children to represent the two groups with double-sided counters or counters in two colours that can be placed in a ten frame. It is important to spend time mastering these steps to embed and strengthen understanding of the composition of 10.

In Question ❶, draw out that the bottles on the wall are one group and the bottles on the floor are another group. Ash's question is an important prompt to help children to realise that a full ten frame always holds 10, no matter what the combination of red and yellow counters.

ASK

- Question ❶: *What can you see here? How many bottles are on the wall? Can you see another group?* [Bottles on the floor.] *How could you show how many are in each group? How many bottles are in each group?*

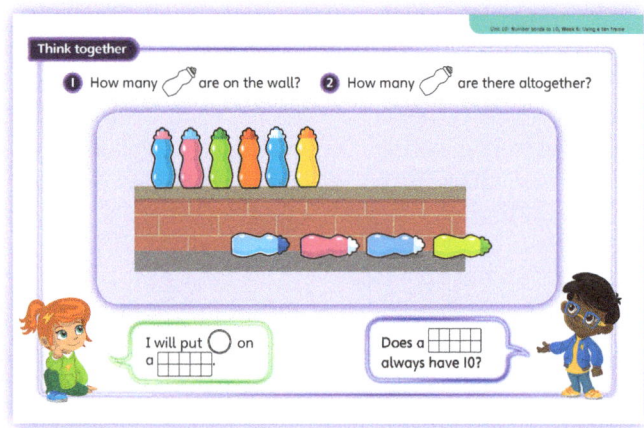

- Question ❷: *What could you use to help you count all of the bottles? Can you show this on a ten frame? Can you see how many altogether?*
- Question ❷: Refer to Ash's question. *If a ten frame is full, will it always show 10?*

DEEPEN Extend thinking from Ash's question using the **Ten frame teaching tool**. Fill the ten frame with 10 counters in two colours. Ask: *How many?* Next, remove a counter. Ask: *Is this still 10? Why not? How do you know?* Repeat the activity using various combinations of counters, sometimes showing 10 to ensure children are confident that a full ten frame shows 10 and a ten frame that is not full will always show less than 10.

Practice: Journal 1

WAYS OF WORKING Independent thinking

IN FOCUS The focus of this **Practice** activity is to reinforce and embed the two-step method laid out in **Discover** and **Share**, and practised in **Think together**, to support children when working out how many altogether, based on number bonds to 10. The composition of 10 is a key learning objective to master in this unit.

MASTERY CHECKPOINT Children who have mastered this concept can identify pairs of numbers that make 10, confidently using the two-step method of combining number bonds to 10 and counting and/or showing them in a ten frame to accurately work out how many altogether.

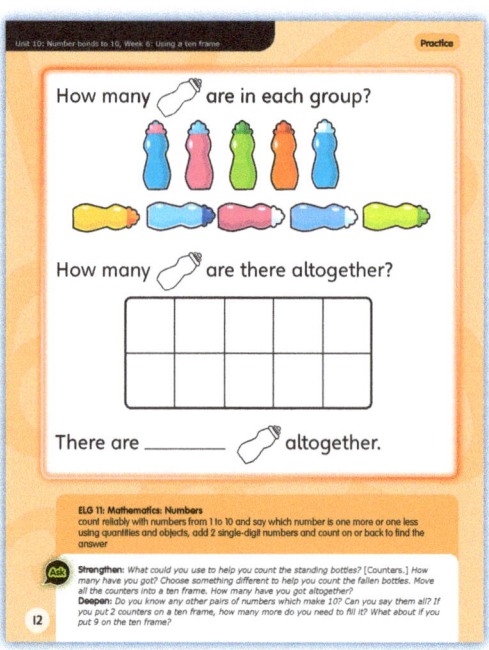

Day 4

Learning focus
Using knowledge of number bonds to 10 to work out how many more

Challenge

WAYS OF WORKING Whole class or small groups

IN FOCUS This **Challenge** activity requires children to find a missing number in the context of bonds to 10. Children will need to use the knowledge they have built up, that a full ten frame always totals 10, and begin to be able to use number bonds to 10 flexibly. If children need a starting point, remind them of the two-step method they have been using with counters and a ten frame.

ASK
- *What can you see in the picture?*
- *What can you use to represent the bottles?* [Counters.]
- Refer children to what Flo is saying. *Do you think a ten frame can help you? How?*
- *Now you can see how many bottles you have, how many more do you need to make 10? How many empty spaces are there in the ten frame?*

STRENGTHEN For children who are finding it hard to visualise the concept of missing numbers and 'how many more', use yellow counters in the ten frame to represent what is missing. Showing children a complete ten frame, with 7 red counters representing the bottles in the picture, and 3 yellow counters representing the missing amount, will help children to see what is missing, and therefore 'how many more' are needed to make 10.

DEEPEN Help to embed understanding of the concept of missing numbers by varying the amounts shown in the ten frame. Use the **Ten frame teaching tool** to display a number of red counters, asking: *How many counters are shown here? How many more do you need to make 10?* Repeat this, each time using a different number of red counters in the ten frame.

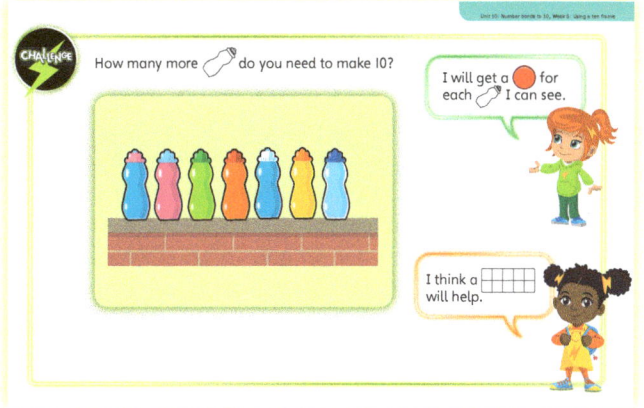

GET ACTIVE Children roll a dice to see how many counters they can put in the ten frame and then work out how many more they need to fill the ten frame. How many different pairs of numbers can they find to make 10? Allow children to use 10 counters for support where necessary. Children can also use bead strings to explore number bonds to 10, hiding some beads and getting a partner to say how many are hidden.

Unit 10: Number bonds to 10, Week 6: Using a ten frame

Day 5

Learning focus
Consolidating number bonds to 10

Practical activities

WAYS OF WORKING Whole class
Display the number bonds rhyme to provide support for children who need it.

IN FOCUS Children should now be getting more familiar with the pairs of numbers which make 10 and be relying less on counting. This group activity will help to develop quick recall. Having the number bonds rhyme displayed will support those children still needing to check.

GET ACTIVE Number bonds rhyme
Chant the rhyme together, encouraging children to show each number with their fingers

5 and 5 they add to 10,
6 and 4 make 10 again.
7 and 3, they make 10 too,
Guess what? So do 8 and 2.
9 and 1, 10 and 0,
Learn them all, be a number bond hero.

Pairs to 10
Give each child a digit card to 10 and ask them to find their number-bond partner (for example, the child with 6 finds the child with 4). Pair children up to provide some peer support, where necessary. Once children have found their partners, they can sit down together.

10 fingers
Show children a number on your fingers, saying the number aloud. Children show the number which goes with it to make 10. For example, if you show and say 9, children show and say 1.

Reflect: Journal 2

WAYS OF WORKING Independent thinking

IN FOCUS This **Reflect** activity gives children the opportunity to show they have understood and are confident with what they have learnt. Encourage children to make or draw number bonds to 10 in a way that they choose. This could include placing, or drawing, real life objects in the ten frame, or placing then drawing counters in the ten frame. Use the question prompts at the bottom of the page to give children a starting point and to encourage them to show all possible number bonds to 10.

MASTERY CHECKPOINT **Children who have mastered this concept** can represent number bonds to 10 in a variety of ways and, with some support, can use ten frames to help them work out how many altogether and how many more.

Children who have not yet mastered this concept can represent some number bonds to 10 but need support when deciding which number bonds to represent and prompts for how to represent them.

Children who have mastered this concept with greater depth can confidently show all number bonds to 10, demonstrate the two-step approach for working out how many altogether, and can use a ten frame to help them work out how many more to make 10.

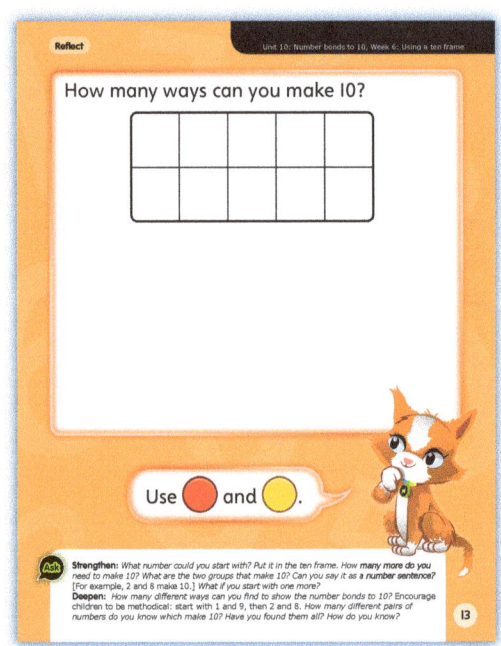

69

Unit 10: Number bonds to 10, Week 7: The part-whole model to 10

The part-whole model to 10

Learning focus
This week, children will explore all the different ways to make 10 on a part-whole model, and gain confidence with the concept and vocabulary of *parts* and *wholes*: that the whole can be made up of two or more parts, and that the parts are combined to make the whole.

Small steps
- Previous step: Using a ten frame
- **This step: The part-whole model to 10**
- Next step: Spatial awareness

COMMON MISCONCEPTIONS

Children may not see that the whole is the sum of the parts. Using counters, encourage children to lay the number in each part out in a long line or in a ten frame to compare the sum of the two parts with the total in the whole. Ask:
- *How many are in each part? How many are there altogether? What do you notice?*

Children may use a random approach to finding number bonds to 10, missing some of them. To encourage a consistent strategy, use a bead string starting with 5 and 5 and moving one bead at a time to show 6 and 4, 7 and 3 and so on. Ask:
- *Can you show me 6 and 4 on the bead string? If you move one bead across, how many will be on that side now? How many will there be on the other side?*

KEY LANGUAGE

In lesson: count, group, counters, how many, altogether, more, each, part-whole model, whole, part

Other language to be used by the teacher: how many more, how many fewer, number bond to 10, bead string, add, one more, one less

STRUCTURES AND REPRESENTATIONS

part-whole model, counters

RESOURCES

Mandatory: counters in two colours, blank part-whole model, multilink cubes

Optional: bead strings, 0–10 digit cards, buttons, paper plates, glue, paper shapes, hula hoops, bean bags, small part-whole models (photocopiable 11), toy fish, bowls

EXPLORE

Taking every opportunity throughout the school day to build and reinforce mathematical concepts gives children's learning purpose and meaning in the wider context of their lives.

ACTIVITY	AREA	DESCRIPTION	RESOURCES
Bead strings	Classroom	In pairs, children use a bead string to show and record all the number bonds to 10. They should start with 10 and 0, move one bead to show 9 and 1 then 8 and 2. Continue to 1 and 9 and finally 0 and 10. They can record each bond using digit cards.	Bead strings, 0–10 digit cards
Hoops	Outside or hall	Give pairs or small groups of children 10 bean bags and 2 hoops. They take turns to throw the bean bags into either hula hoop until all the bean bags are in the hoops. They use digit cards to record the number bond shown. Repeat.	Hula hoops, bean bags, 0–10 digit cards
Plates of fish	Art area	Give pairs of children 3 plates and some shapes to stick on to represent the fish. They make a part-whole model to show a bond to 10 in the two parts and 10 in the whole. Use to make a display.	Paper plates, glue, paper shapes

Unit 10: Number bonds to 10, Week 7: The part-whole model to 10

Day 1

Learning focus
Composition of 10

Before you teach
- Can children count up to 10 objects?
- Do children understand that numbers can be partitioned into pairs or groups of smaller numbers?
- Can children show a bond to 10 on a ten frame using two colours of counters?

Starter

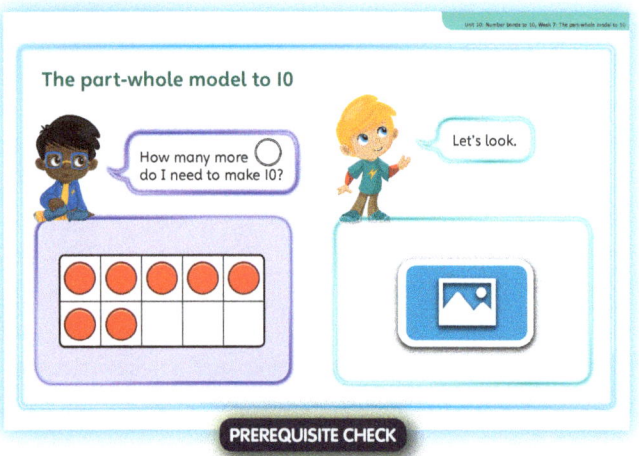

PREREQUISITE CHECK

PREREQUISITE CHECK Horizontal ten frame with 7 counters in and 3 empty spaces.

WAYS OF WORKING Whole class

IN FOCUS Children use knowledge of number bonds and ten frames to determine how many more counters are needed to make 10.

ASK
- How many counters are in the ten frame? Do you need to count them all?
- How many counters are in the top row? How do you know?
- How many empty spaces are there? So how many more are needed to make 10?
- When you add one more counter to this ten frame, how many more do you need to fill it now?
- If you take one counter away, how many more do you need to fill it now?

STIMULUS

STIMULUS Photograph to prompt an activity. The photograph shows a child with 8 fingers up and 2 fingers folded over to show the number bond 8 and 2 or 2 and 8.

WAYS OF WORKING Whole class

Children can use their fingers to represent the number bonds but, if they need to, could use counters or a stick of multilink cubes.

IN FOCUS This **Stimulus** prompts an activity using fingers to reinforce number bonds to 10. Discuss what children can see in the photograph, asking them to show this with their own fingers or counters. Ensure that children understand that the child in the photograph has 10 fingers so is showing a number bond to 10. Encourage children to say what they see as a number bond to 10: *8 and 2 make 10*. Ask children to show a different pair of numbers and to say the bond to 10.

ASK
- How many fingers are pointing up? How many fingers are folded down?
- How many fingers are there altogether? How can you say this? [8 and 2 make 10]
- When 3 fingers are up, how many will be folded down?

GET ACTIVE Children play with a partner, taking it in turns to show a number bond on their fingers or using counters. The partner should say what they see: *7 fingers up and 3 fingers down is 10 fingers altogether*. Children who need to can count the folded fingers, but some may be starting to learn the number bonds and be able to answer without counting. They could also complete the bond: one child shows a number 0–10 and other child shows how many complete to 10.

Unit 10: Number bonds to 10, Week 7: The part-whole model to 10

Day 2

Learning focus
Using the part-whole model to break 10 into two parts

Discover

WAYS OF WORKING Whole class or small groups

IN FOCUS The **Discover** is set in an aquatic shop, which will be the focus for the whole week. There are 10 fish in the large tank, showing the number bond 6 and 4. Ensure children understand that Aidan will carry all the red fish home in his bag, and that Ella will carry all the yellow fish in her bag. Encourage any discussion around fairness and whether they should have the same number of fish, always coming back to how many there would be in total (10), to help children explore the different number bonds to 10.

ASK
- *How many fish are in the tank altogether? How do you know?*
- *What could the two parts be?* [yellow fish and red fish]
- *How many fish are in each part?*
- *Aidan wants red fish. How many fish will he get?*
- *Ella wants yellow fish. How many will she get?*

STRENGTHEN To help children to visualise how many fish there are altogether, use red and yellow counters to represent the fish, placing them either in a long line or in a

ten frame on the **Ten frame teaching tool** to show that the total of 6 and 4 is 10.

DEEPEN Ask children to consider there being one less red fish and one more yellow fish. Ask: *Will there still be 10 fish in the tank? How many of each colour fish would there have to be for the twins to get the same number of fish each?*

Share

WAYS OF WORKING Whole class
Ensure counters in two colours and blank part-whole models are available.

IN FOCUS The focus of **Share** is to represent the number bond of 6 and 4 in a part-whole model, shown by the tank and the two bags of water used to carry the fish home safely. The progression from concrete to pictorial is shown by representing the fish in the tank (concrete) with counters in a part-whole model (pictorial). Having the counters set up in a dice pattern can help children start to subitise. Use the **Part whole teaching tool** to model placing the counters into the parts and the whole, and to show the numerals.

ASK
- *What are the parts? Can you count them?*
- *Are there more yellow fish or more red fish? Who wants yellow fish? Who wants red fish?*
- *Who will get more fish, Aidan or Ella?*
- *How many more fish will Aidan have than Ella?*
- *What are the bags of water for? Why do they need to take the fish home in bags of water?*
- *How many fish will be left in the tank if Mum buys 10?*

STRENGTHEN Encourage children to play with a part-whole model, first showing the two separate parts using red and yellow counters as in **Share**, then combining them into the whole. *Are there still the same amount of counters? How many?*

Encourage children to say the number bond: *6 and 4 make 10.* Ask children to swap the parts around. Ask: *Are there still 10? What is this number bond? 4 and 6 make 10.* The **Part whole teaching tool** can also be used.

DEEPEN Ask children to use a part-whole model to show that 6 and 4 has the same total as 4 and 6. Can they show a different inverse pair, such as 8 and 2 with 2 and 8? Provide copies of small part-whole models (photocopiable 11) for them to record the bonds they find.

GET ACTIVE Play the Hoops game from **Explore** (page 70). Can children start by showing the number bond 6 and 4 first?

72

Unit 10: Number bonds to 10, Week 7: The part-whole model to 10

Day 3

Learning focus

Identifying whole and parts when variation is a factor

Think together

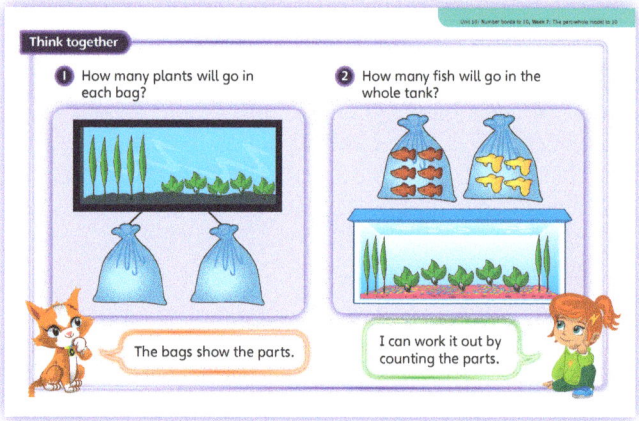

WAYS OF WORKING Whole class

Ensure that two colours of counters and blank part-whole models are available for children to use today, to support their answers. Use single page mode to view the flashcard to help children focus on each question.

IN FOCUS In Question ❶, the whole is broken into two parts, where both parts have an equal number of plants if they are split by the type of plant (as shown in the picture).
In Question ❷, different parts (the fish) are put back together into a whole. Reinforce this using the **Part whole teaching tool**, and demonstrate breaking a whole into parts, then combining the parts back into the whole and recounting.

ASK

- Question ❶: *What can you see here? What is the same and what is different about the plants? How could you break the plants into two parts? If you break the plants like this (by plant type), how many will go in each bag?*
- Question ❷: *What can you see here? How many fish are in each bag? What will happen if both the bags (both parts) are emptied into one tank (the whole)? Where will all the fish go? How many fish will go in the whole tank?*

STRENGTHEN Ask children to put a set of 10 counters in the whole of a blank part-whole model, break them up into two parts, then recombine them into the whole to check that there are still 10.

DEEPEN Ask children if the plants could be broken up in a different way. They may need reassurance that the plants do not have to be divided by type.

Practice: Journal 1

WAYS OF WORKING Independent thinking

IN FOCUS The focus of this **Practice** activity is to reinforce that 7 and 3 make 10 using two colours of fish, 7 red and 3 yellow. This is the same bond children met in the **Prerequisite check** on a ten frame, but now it is shown on fish tanks in the same formation as a part-whole model. Encourage children to think about how they will break the fish into two smaller tanks (parts). Remind children that it is the same number bond, however it is shown.

MASTERY CHECKPOINT Children who have mastered this concept can confidently break a whole to 10 into two parts, where the two parts have been clearly differentiated by colour.

Unit 10: Number bonds to 10, Week 7: The part-whole model to 10

Day 4

Learning focus
Using number bonds to 10 to break a whole into parts

Challenge

WAYS OF WORKING Whole class or small groups

IN FOCUS This **Challenge** encourages children to explore all the options for number bonds to 10. The whole shows 10 identical fish in a ten-frame layout, so that children can identify quickly that the total is 10. There are no clues as to how the fish should be broken into the two empty tanks, so encourage children to find all the ways to break the whole into two parts.

ASK
- *What can you see in the picture? What do you notice about the fish?*
- *How could you break the fish into two groups?*
- *How can you make sure you have found all the possible ways?*
- *If there are 8 in this tank, how many will go in this tank? If you put 8 in the other tank, can you say without counting how many will go in this tank?*
- *Is it possible to have the same number of fish in each tank?*

STRENGTHEN Children work in a small group with an adult. They have 10 toy fish to put into two bowls. Give them a methodical starting point for each number bond (using physical objects). Ask: *If 9 go in this bowl, how many will be in this bowl?* Record the bond using digit cards. *If 8 go in this bowl, how many will be in this bowl?* Remember to include 10 and 0.

DEEPEN Children draw their own part-whole models to show all the bonds to 10 or use small blank part-whole models (photocopiable 11). They can use blank part-whole models to manipulate 10 counters if necessary. Ask: *Have you found all the possible pairs to 10? How can you check? If there are 0 counters in one part, what will be in the other part? Can you show the part-whole models with numerals as well?*

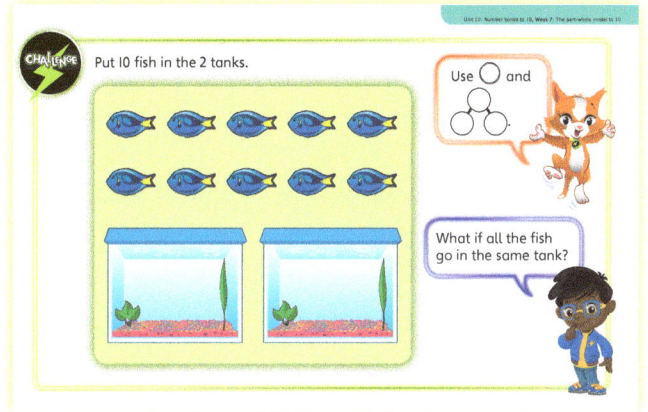

GET ACTIVE Attach large 0–10 digit cards to the board and ask pairs of children to choose numbers that show a bond to 10.

Day 5

> **Learning focus**
> Exploring all the different number bonds to 10 to consolidate understanding

Practical activities

WAYS OF WORKING Whole class

IN FOCUS Encourage children to recall the number bonds to 10 rather than having to count.

GET ACTIVE **Number bond matching**
Children take it in turns to call out a number from 0 to 10. The class responds with the number bond to 10. For example, a child calls out '4' and the class responds with '6'. Give all children a chance to think before asking them to respond after you say *ready, steady, go* or similar. Avoid leading in with the numbers 1, 2, 3 as these numbers may or may not be the answer!

Ten!
Using large digit cards 0–10, show pairs of numbers. When children spot a bond to 10, they stand up or shout '10'.

Reflect: Journal 2

WAYS OF WORKING Independent thinking
Have buttons or counters available.

IN FOCUS This **Reflect** activity gives children the opportunity to explore all the number bonds to 10 again. They should first count out 10 buttons or objects from a larger group to represent the buttons, to help them with the activity and to practise their counting skills, and place one on top of each item in the picture. When children have moved the buttons into the bowls, reassure them that the whole is still 10 – there is the same number of buttons, but they have been moved into the two parts. Moving them back into the whole should reinforce the concept of the whole being the total of the parts.

MASTERY CHECKPOINT **Children who have mastered this concept** can confidently represent number bonds to 10 in a part-whole model and understand that the whole is the total of the parts.

Children who have not yet mastered this concept can say or work out some number bonds to 10 but may need support to represent them in a part-whole model.

Children who have mastered this concept with greater depth can confidently show all number bonds to 10, showing them as part-whole models. They will begin to use a more systematic approach to show that they have found all the ways to do this.

Unit 11
Shape and space

Mastery Expert tip! "Providing children with a range of 3D shapes and objects, plus images of 2D shapes in different orientations, helped strengthen their understanding of the shapes and prompted them to start to describe the properties."

Don't forget to watch the Shape and space video!

ELGs

This unit supports the following ELGs:

→ **ELG 4: Physical development: Moving and handling**
move confidently in a range of ways, safely negotiating space

→ **ELG 12: Mathematics: Shape, space and measures**
use everyday language to talk about size, weight, capacity, position, distance, time and money to compare quantities and objects and to solve problems
explore characteristics of everyday objects and shapes and use mathematical language to describe them

→ **ELG 14: Understanding the world: The world**
know about similarities and differences in relation to places, objects, materials and living things
talk about the features of their own immediate environment and how environments might vary from one another

→ **ELG 15: Understanding the world: Technology**
select and use technology for particular purposes

WHY THIS UNIT IS IMPORTANT

This unit introduces positional language and the names and some of the key properties of common 2D and 3D shapes. These are important building blocks for the concepts of shape and space children will meet later in KS1 and KS2. Spatial awareness supports all aspects of maths and familiarity with shape builds confidence prior to using the mathematical properties and language met in KS1.

WAYS OF WORKING

Ensure the environment encourages children to use the language introduced on an everyday basis. At tidy-up time encourage the use of positional language to describe where objects go and whether they can be stacked. Signs in the construction area and modelling area can help children to think about which 3D shapes they are choosing to build with. 3D shapes in the painting area can encourage children to think about the 2D shapes they can print.

WHERE THIS UNIT FITS

→ Unit 10: Number bonds to 10
→ **Unit 11: Shape and space**
→ Unit 12: Exploring patterns

In this unit, the focus is on the key language related to shape and space. Children start by using positional and directional language before moving on to describing and comparing 3D and 2D shapes. Children will be introduced to shapes and their properties with a focus on rolling and stacking with 3D shapes and viewing 2D shapes in different orientations.

Link to Key Stage 1

Geometry – properties of shape

Unit 5: 2D and 3D shape
- recognise and name common 2D and 3D shapes, including: 2D shapes [for example, rectangles (including squares), circles and triangles]; 3D shapes [for example, cuboids (including cubes), pyramids and spheres]

Geometry – position and direction

Unit 15: Position and direction
- describe position, direction and movement, including whole, half, quarter and three-quarter turn

Knowing the names and understanding the properties of 2D and 3D shapes provides a strong foundation for KS1.

Unit 11: Shape and space

ASSESSING MASTERY

Children who have mastered this unit will be able to:
- use positional and directional language to follow and give instructions
- build, describe and sort common 3D shapes (sphere, cylinder, cone, cube, cuboid)
- match 3D shapes to their 2D prints and name each of these regular 2D shapes

COMMON MISCONCEPTIONS	STRENGTHENING UNDERSTANDING	GOING DEEPER
Children may confuse the meaning of the words, such as up and down, below or above, in front of or behind.	Ask children to place objects according to given instructions. Ask children to explain where an object is in relation to other objects.	Ask children to direct each other to place objects in relation to other objects using the key language.
Children may apply the names of 2D shapes to 3D shapes or vice versa. They may also use common objects to describe the shapes rather than the name of the shape.	Encourage the links with real-life objects but repeat the names of the shapes when modelling stem sentences to describe the shapes.	Ask children to find what shapes have in common as well as their differences. They can use everyday language to highlight the similarities and differences.
Children may fail to recognise a shape when its orientation changes, and may focus on superficial differences such as colour or size.	Ensure that you present shapes in lots of orientations around the classroom environment. Once children have identified a shape, rotate it and say: *I wonder if it is still a …*	Show a shape and name it, rotate the shape and use a puppet to suggest that the shape has changed and it's not the same anymore. Ask children to explain to the puppet why it is the same shape.

STRUCTURES AND REPRESENTATIONS

2D and 3D shapes: It is important that children have a range of 2D and 3D shapes to manipulate and explore. These should include: cube, cuboid, cylinder, cone, circle, triangle, square, rectangle.

RESOURCES

Mandatory: teddy, range of everyday objects (including some that are 2D and 3D shapes), 3D shapes (cubes, cuboids, cones, cylinders, spheres), 2D shapes (circles, squares, rectangles, triangles), building blocks, empty boxes, paint, potatoes, pictures of 2D shapes, including shapes in the everyday environment (photocopiables 15 and 16)

Optional: box for treasure chest, boxes to hide things in or on, paper and pencils, doll's house and furniture, play people, PE equipment (mats, benches, hula hoops), toy bed, toy car, bean bags, teddies, construction bricks or recycled material, sticky tape, glue, chalk, programmable toy or remote control car, real-life 3D shapes (cones, spheres, cubes, cuboids and cylinders), cones, balls, bricks, crawling tubes, small soft balls, paper tubes, boxes, cartons, playdough, outdoor slide or slope, feely bag, sand or foam, tools for mark marking, camera, drawing materials, lolly sticks or string, postitional language flash cards (photocopiable 12), arrows (photocopiable 13), 3D shapes (photocopiable 14)

TEACHING TOOLS

2D shapes, 3D shapes

KEY LANGUAGE

There is some key language that children will need to know as part of the learning in this unit:
- **in**, **on**, **below**, **under**, above, in front of, behind, next to
- **up**, **down**, **across**, forwards, backwards, left, right
- **roll**, **stack**, **push**, **curved**, **straight**, **round**,
- **corners**, face, edge, sides
- **square**, **rectangle**, **circle**, **triangle**
- sphere, cube, cuboid, cylinder, cone
- big, little, flat, like a box, like a can, slides, pointy
- odd one out, same, difference, different properties, characteristics

Unit 11: Shape and space, Week 8: Spatial awareness

Spatial awareness

Learning focus
This week, children will develop their vocabulary to describe the position of objects. They will look at items from different viewpoints and draw representations of the items they see.

Small steps
→ Previous step: The part-whole model to 10
→ **This step: Spatial awareness**
→ Next step: 3D shapes

COMMON MISCONCEPTIONS
Children may confuse the meaning of the words, such as up and down, below or above, in front of or behind. Repetition and use of the language in practical activities is key to understanding. Ask:
- *Do you need to climb up or down these steps? Can you put the teddy in front of the mat or behind the chair or under the table?*

KEY LANGUAGE
In lesson: in, on, below, under, up, down, across, difference

Other language to be used by the teacher: left, right, above, same, in front of, behind, next to, forwards, backwards

RESOURCES
Mandatory: teddy, range of everyday objects to demonstrate positional language

Optional: box for treasure chest, boxes to hide things in or on, paper, pencil, doll's house and furniture, play people, PE equipment (mats, benches, hula hoops), toy bed, toy car, bean bags, teddies, construction bricks or recycled material, sticky tape, glue, chalk, programmable toy or remote control car, recording equipment, positional language flashcards (photocopiable 12), large arrows (photocopiable 13)

EXPLORE

Taking every opportunity throughout the school day to build and reinforce mathematical concepts gives children's learning purpose and meaning in the wider context of their lives.

ACTIVITY	AREA	DESCRIPTION	RESOURCES
Treasure hunt	Classroom	Show children a small 'treasure chest' and ask a child to hide it somewhere in the classroom. They then give instructions to another child, who finds it. Other children draw a map to show the way to the treasure.	Box for a treasure chest, paper, pencils
Doll's house	Classroom	Empty the doll's house and ask children to redesign the rooms following some key instructions that could be given by a teacher or a recorded message, for example: *The bedroom is above the kitchen. There is a person on the bed. There is a lamp behind the settee.*	Doll's house and furniture, play people
Obstacle course	Outside	Challenge children to create an obstacle course in the outdoor area. They model how to use the course, using key language: *under the boxes, through the tunnel, over the bench.*	PE equipment (mats, benches, hula hoops)

Unit 11: Shape and space, Week 8: Spatial awareness

Day 1

Learning focus

Understanding positional and directional language in practical contexts

Before you teach

- Can children follow a set of simple instructions?
- Can children follow instructions using simple positional language?
- How can you use positional language in everyday tasks to reinforce its use?

Starter

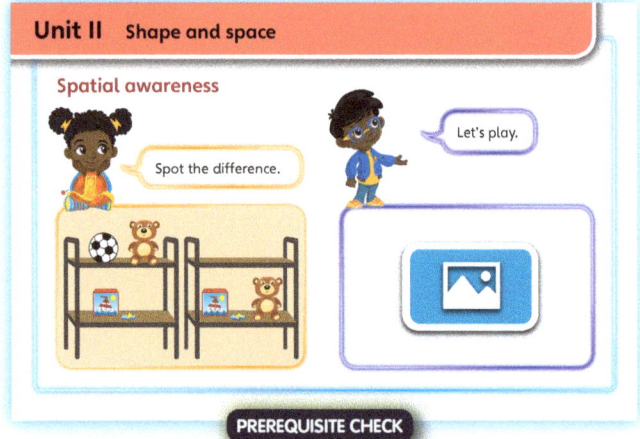

PREREQUISITE CHECK

PREREQUISITE CHECK Children look at two pictures to see what is the same and what is different about them.

WAYS OF WORKING Whole class

IN FOCUS Children use their observation skills to find the differences between two pictures. Can they spot which item is missing (football) and which has moved places (teddy) in the second picture?

ASK
- What items are **on** the shelves?
- What is the same about the pictures? Which item has not moved?
- What is **different** about the pictures? Are there the same number of items?
- Has the teddy moved up or down? Which item is missing?

STIMULUS

STIMULUS Photograph prompting a guided activity

WAYS OF WORKING Small groups

In advance, hide teddies in various places around the classroom or outside area for children to find.

IN FOCUS Children go on a bear hunt to find teddies. Give clues, modelling positional language (*behind, on, in, under*) to support children in finding the teddies.

ASK
- Is the teddy **under** the table? Is the teddy **on** the table?
- Walk **across** the classroom to look **behind** the blinds. Is the teddy there?
- Is the teddy **in** the box? Can you put teddy **under** the cover/ **on** the book?

GET ACTIVE Continue the bear hunt activity: encourage a child to hide a teddy and give the other children clues to find it. If there are enough teddies, let children work in pairs, taking it in turns to hide the teddy.

Day 2

Learning focus

Using positional language to describe the position of items (1)

Discover

WAYS OF WORKING Whole class or small groups
Provide opportunities to link to the small world area and doll's house in the classroom. Use every opportunity to reinforce the use of positional language in everyday contexts. For example, ask children where certain key objects are, and model and encourage full sentence responses using the key positional language of *in, on, under, above, below, next to* and *behind*.

IN FOCUS Children use positional language to describe where the rooms and furniture in the doll's house are, in relation to the other rooms or items. Can they describe the position of other objects they can see in the picture?

ASK
- Which rooms can you see in the house? How can you tell that this is a bedroom/kitchen?
- Which items can you see in the kitchen/bedroom/living room/bathroom?
- Which room is below the bedroom? Which room is above the kitchen?

- What is on the bed? What is on top of your bed?
- What do you put in the oven/in the sink?

GET ACTIVE Provide a doll's house, furniture and play people. Encourage children to set up the doll's house and place a play person inside. They use positional language to describe to a partner where the person is.

Share

WAYS OF WORKING Whole class

IN FOCUS Children use positional language to describe the position of the teddy.

ASK
- Which room is the teddy in?
- Is the teddy **in** the bed, **on** the bed or **under** the bed?

STRENGTHEN Use a teddy or doll and a toy bed to model the difference between *in* the bed, *on* the bed and *under* the bed. You could also model *in, on, under* and *behind* using a toy car in the outdoor area.

DEEPEN Put a teddy on a chair. Ask children: *Where is the teddy? Is the teddy in the chair, on the chair or under the chair? Can you put the teddy under the chair? Can you put the teddy in the chair? Is this possible? Can you put teddy next to or behind the chair?*

GET ACTIVE Use mats, benches and hoops in a large space. Call out instructions for children to follow, for example: *Stand on the mat, sit in the hoop, stand behind or in front of the bench, lie under the mat.* Children can then create their own instructions for other children to follow.

Unit 11: Shape and space, Week 8: Spatial awareness

Day 3

Learning focus

Using positional language to describe the position of items (2)

Think together

WAYS OF WORKING Whole class
Consider using recording equipment to record key vocabulary to support children in their descriptions of positions.

IN FOCUS Question ❶ builds on **Discover** and **Share**, using the language of *in* and *on*. Question ❷ develops language further, introducing *under*, *below* and *behind*.

ASK

- Question ❶: *What are the flowers in? What are the flowers on?*
- Question ❷: *Can you use 'in' and 'on' to describe the ball? What words do you need to describe where the ball is?*
- Question ❷: *Can you describe where the ball is in relation to where the wellies are? Is the ball in front of or behind the wellies?*

STRENGTHEN Give children a bean bag each and show them one of the positional language flashcards (photocopiable 12). Children should use the bean bag to demonstrate the positional language shown on the card, for example, if you show 'under' children should place the bean bag *under* something.

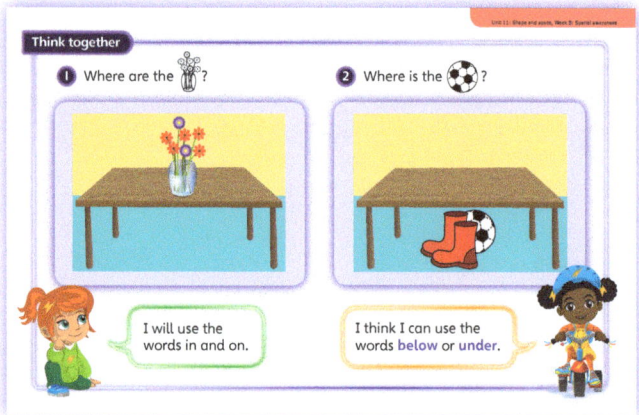

DEEPEN Give children a bean bag each and **two** words to describe the position of the bean bag, such as *in* and *under*. Children position the bean bag using the given words. Ask children to describe the position of the bean bag in a full sentence, for example: The bean bag is *in* a box, *under* the table. Children will need to be creative to show combinations of under and above; in and on; behind and in front of.

Practice: Journal 1

WAYS OF WORKING Independent thinking

IN FOCUS Children consider how viewpoint affects what can be seen. They continue to use positional language to explain why the teddy can or cannot see different objects. Help children to begin to understand that you cannot see things behind you without altering your own position (turning your head or your body).

MASTERY CHECKPOINT Children can understand that things can be seen that are in front of you or to the side of you. They can describe the position of objects in relation to other objects.

81

Day 4

> **Learning focus**
> Describing movement using the language up, down and across

Challenge

WAYS OF WORKING Whole class or in pairs
Have large arrows (photocopiable 13) ready to support children's understanding of different directions.

IN FOCUS Children use directional language to describe a route. Children are encouraged to use the language *up*, *down* and *across* to describe movement.

ASK
- *Which way will Ella go on the ladder?*
- *Could you trace a line to help you find the way?*
- *Does Ella need to go up or down? Could you use left and right to describe direction as well?*

STRENGTHEN Play a game of Snakes and Ladders. Explain how the game works, that children should zigzag across the board, following the numbers to the right and sometimes to the left. If they land at the bottom of the ladder, they go up it, if they land on the top of a snake, they slide down it. Encourage children to explain how they are moving: up, down or across.

DEEPEN Take children on a walk around school and the playground. Encourage children to think about what they can travel up or down (steps, a slope) and when they can move across. If appropriate, encourage children to think about left and right or forwards and backwards. Can they follow a set of instructions? For example: *Go up the steps, walk forward 5 steps, go across the playground, turn right.* When back in the classroom, ask children to draw out the route and explain where they have been to other children using the key positional language.

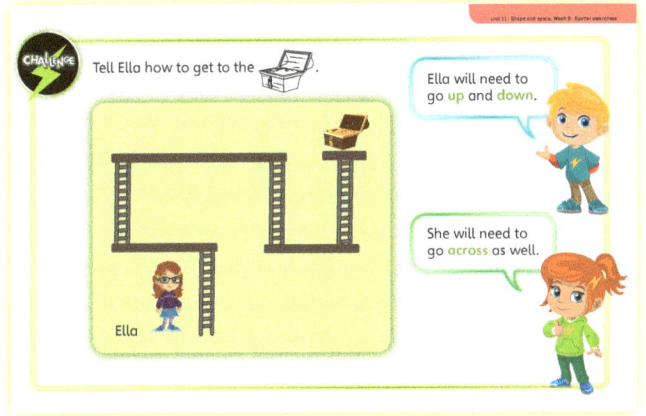

GET ACTIVE Sing the song, *The Grand Old Duke of York*. Model actions for 'up' and 'down' to be used in the song. As a class, come up with actions for other directions, such as behind, in front of, above, below. Ask: *Can you think of any other songs or rhymes where you could use these actions?*

Unit 11: Shape and space, Week 8: Spatial awareness

Day 5

Learning focus
Using directional and positional language to describe a route

Practical activities

WAYS OF WORKING Whole class

IN FOCUS Children use positional and directional language in a range of contexts and start to understand that sometimes the language used is dependent on your viewpoint or the direction you are facing at the start.

GET ACTIVE **Model building**
Children make a model using construction bricks or recycled material and use positional language to describe where the different parts are in relation to each other. Encourage children to make a model to show in or on, under or above, behind or in front of and next to. Can they hide something so that it can only be seen from the top or from the back?

Map making
Children make a map to show a route through the playground. They swap maps with a partner and follow the route. Ask: *What will you see at different points? Can you draw what you can see?*

Treasure hunt
Ask some children to hide some treasure in the classroom. They draw a map or give clear instructions to their partners to find the treasure.

Forward and backwards
Draw a chalk maze on the playground, directing children to move forwards or backwards, left or right, to find their way through it. Alternatively use a programmable toy or remote control car to follow the maze.

Reflect: Journal 2

WAYS OF WORKING Independent thinking

IN FOCUS Children trace then draw a route and use directional language to describe it. Prompt children to realise that there is more than one route and ask them to explain the similarities and differences between them.

MASTERY CHECKPOINT **Children who have mastered this concept** can use positional and directional language to follow and give instructions.

Children who have not yet mastered this concept can use some positional and directional language and follow instructions using this language.

Children who have mastered this concept with greater depth can use positional and directional language to follow and give instructions. They can understand that language will change depending on viewpoint and the direction you are facing when you start to move.

83

Unit 11: Shape and space, Week 9: 3D shapes

3D shapes

Learning focus
This week, children will focus on properties of 3D shapes through hands on exploration and play.

Small steps
→ Previous step: Spatial awareness
→ **This step: 3D shapes**
→ Next step: 2D shapes

COMMON MISCONCEPTIONS
Children may use the names of 2D shapes for 3D shapes or vice versa. Children may name a shape as a familiar object, such as calling a sphere a ball. Encourage children to make links to real life objects but focus on a shape being **like a** familiar object rather than the same thing: *Like a ball.* Ask:
- *What does this shape look like? What is its special maths name?*

Children may fail to recognise a shape when its orientation changes, and may focus on superficial differences such as colour or size. It is important they see shapes in many orientations. Ask:
- *If you turn it this way, do you know what it is called now? Is it still the same shape if you turn it back this way?*

KEY LANGUAGE
In lesson: roll, stack, curved, push

Other language to be used by the teacher: sphere, cube, cuboid, cylinder, cone, big, little, round, flat, like a box, like a can, slides, pointy, corner, face, edges

RESOURCES
Mandatory: 3D shapes (cubes, cuboids, cones, cylinders, spheres), building blocks, empty boxes

Optional: real-life 3D shapes (cones, spheres, cubes, cuboids and cylinders), cones, balls, bricks, crawling tubes, small soft balls, paper tubes, boxes, cartons, playdough, hula hoop or chalk, outdoor slide or slope, feely bag, 2D representations of 3D shapes (photocopiable 14)

EXPLORE

Taking every opportunity throughout the school day to build and reinforce mathematical concepts gives children's learning purpose and meaning in the wider context of their lives.

ACTIVITY	AREA	DESCRIPTION	RESOURCES
Building towers	Classroom	Ask children to decide which are the best shapes to use to build the tallest tower.	3D shapes
Obstacle course	Outside	Help children to complete an obstacle course that uses 3D shapes: rolling balls around cones, hopping over bricks, crawling through cylinder tubes.	Cones, balls, bricks, crawling tubes
Bowling	Outside or hall	Set up a bowling game using a variety of 3D recycled materials. Which shapes fall over easily? Which shapes are harder to make fall over?	Small soft balls, paper tubes, boxes and cartons
Playdough shapes	Art area	Children make their own models using playdough. Which are the easiest to make? Which are harder to make?	Playdough

Unit 11: Shape and space, Week 9: 3D shapes

Day 1

Learning focus

Exploring properties of everyday shapes

Starter

PREREQUISITE CHECK

Before you teach

- What words are children using to describe 3D shapes?
- Can children see similarities and differences between 3D shapes?
- Introduce words and phrases to help children describe 3D shapes: big, little, round, flat, like a box, like a can, can roll, can stack, rolls, slides, pointy, corners, etc.

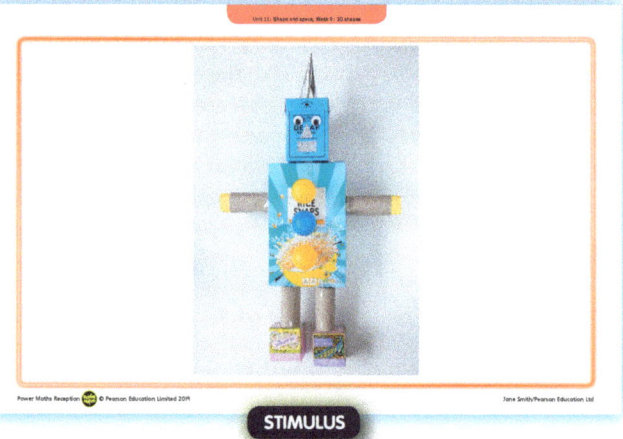

STIMULUS

PREREQUISITE CHECK Describing a picture using positional language: *on top of*, *below*, *behind* and *in front of*.

WAYS OF WORKING Whole class

Have the range of 3D shapes used in this **Prerequisite check** available for children to see and touch.

IN FOCUS Children reinforce their use of positional language from Unit 11, Week 8, to describe the position of an object in relation to other objects. The picture shows everyday 3D objects to prompt discussion and introduce the focus for the week.

ASK

- Where is the football? What is it on top of? What is it behind?
- What is in front of the football? What is below the football?
- Where is the cone?

STIMULUS Photograph to prompt a guided activity

WAYS OF WORKING Whole class or small groups

IN FOCUS Children look at the photograph of the robot made from recycled material and consider the 3D shapes they can see. They use their own familiar vocabulary to describe the shapes as well as being introduced to more mathematical vocabulary.

ASK

- What objects can you see?
- Can you see any curved objects?
- Which shape is on top of the model? What shapes are at the bottom of the model?

GET ACTIVE Using the photograph as a stimulus, encourage children to make their own models from everyday objects. They could work in small groups, thinking about which objects they want to use. Encourage them to use a variety of differently shaped objects to make their model and prompt them to describe the objects to a partner.

85

Unit 11: Shape and space, Week 9: 3D shapes

Day 2

Learning focus

Describing 3D shapes using their common properties

Discover

WAYS OF WORKING Whole class or small groups
Have various 3D shapes available.

IN FOCUS Children look at familiar 3D shapes and consider whether they roll. It is important to clarify the difference between rolling and sliding. Let children feel the surfaces of those objects that do roll, discussing that there needs to be a curved surface for an object to roll. You should use the correct names for the shapes but children should not be expected to use or remember them.

ASK
- *What are children pushing down the slide? What shapes are they?*
- *Which one do you think will roll? Will they both roll?*
- *What other objects can you see in the picture? What kind of shapes are these?*
- *Are there any other shapes in the picture that would roll down the slide?*

STRENGTHEN Use an outdoor slide, or make a slide like the one in the picture, and replicate the objects from the picture to test which roll. Encourage children to think about how they know if a shape will roll. Children should feel the shapes, looking for curved sides. Ask: *Can you think of any other shapes that will roll?*

DEEPEN Use an outdoor slide or make a slide like the one in the picture. Give each child a container to collect five objects from around the classroom that they think will roll. Encourage children to test out each shape on the slide, sorting the shapes into ones that will roll and ones that will not roll. Ask: *Now can you find shapes that will not roll?* Talk about the similarities and differences between the shapes that do roll and the shapes that do not roll.

Share

WAYS OF WORKING Whole class

IN FOCUS Children look at 3D shapes and describe some of their properties.

ASK
- *Which of the shapes is curved? Do you know the special names for these shapes?*
- *Which real life objects can roll? Do these shapes look like any of those in the picture?*
- *Which shapes slide but do not roll? What is the same about the shapes that slide?*

STRENGTHEN Give children a range of spheres and cubes or cuboids in various sizes. Encourage them to feel the curves on the spheres and the flat faces on the cubes or cuboids. Use a slope outside for children to explore and discover practically that all the spheres roll and all the cuboids either slide or slide when pushed.

DEEPEN Encourage children to consider the other shapes in the **Discover** picture. Ask: *Can you predict which other shapes could roll? Why do balls need to be stored in a box rather than loose?* Together, look around the classroom or PE equipment cupboard to see how different shaped solid objects are stored.

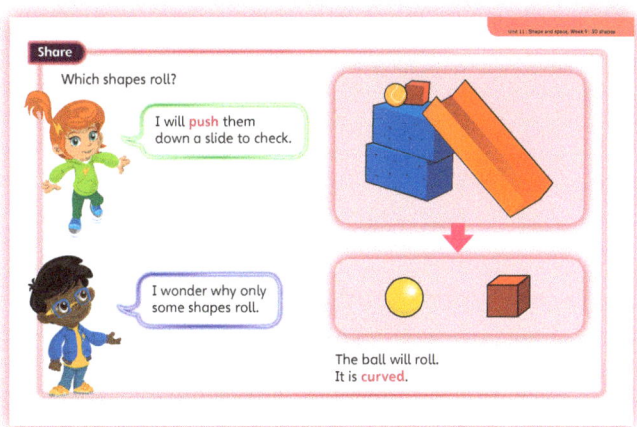

GET ACTIVE Using a hula hoop or chalk circle outside, announce a sorting rule, such as: *They all roll.* Each child should find a shape that matches the rule and run to place it in the hoop. Continue the game, varying the sorting rule each time, for example: *They all slide; they are all flat; they are all curved.*

Day 3

Learning focus

Exploring, describing and comparing the properties of 3D shapes

Think together

WAYS OF WORKING Whole class
Have a range of 3D shapes and objects available for children to use today.

IN FOCUS Children look at a wider range of shapes, considering which roll and which stack. They begin to understand that some objects only roll or stack in certain orientations. If appropriate, explain that each flat surface is called a face.

ASK
- How can you check if the shapes roll? How can you check if the shapes stack?
- Which of the shapes are curved? Which of the shapes are flat? How will pushing them along the floor help you to work this out?
- Do any of the shapes roll **and** stack?

STRENGTHEN Give children a range of 3D shapes and ask them to stack them. Ask: Which shape would you not put on the bottom of the stack? Why? Which shape is a good shape to have at the bottom of a stack? Why? Does this shape also roll?

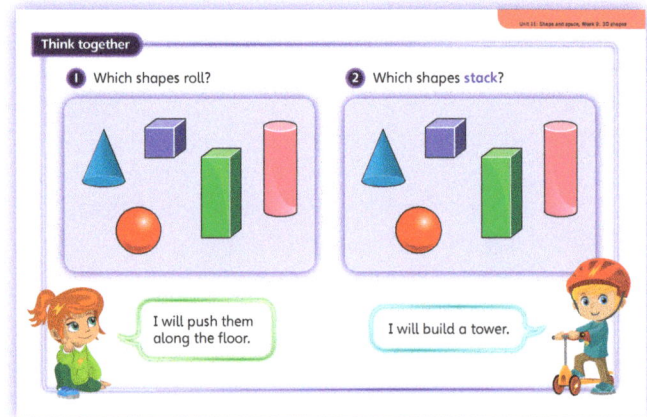

DEEPEN Give children a range of 3D shapes of different sizes. Encourage them to make a stack of shapes. Ask: Which shape did you choose for the bottom of the stack? Why? Why would a small shape not be a good choice for the bottom of a stack? Why would a curved shape not be a good choice? Which shapes can roll and stack? Can you turn the shape around to make it better for stacking or rolling?

Practice: Journal I

WAYS OF WORKING Independent thinking

IN FOCUS Children identify objects that can roll or can stack. They use mathematical vocabulary to describe the shapes.

MASTERY CHECKPOINT Children can use some mathematical properties to describe 3D shapes. They can identify if an object has curved faces and whether it will roll. They can identify shapes that will stack and explain why.

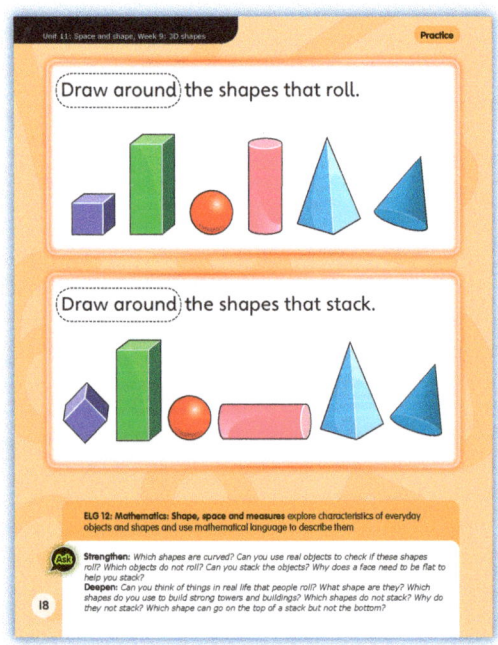

Unit 11: Shape and space, Week 9: 3D shapes

Day 4

Learning focus

Similarities and differences between 3D shapes

Challenge

WAYS OF WORKING Whole class or small groups
Have a variety of 3D shapes available for children to use in this lesson.

IN FOCUS Children decide which shape is the odd one out. There is more than one option, depending on the properties they focus on. Ensure children are familiar with the term *odd one out* and can explain what this means.

ASK
- *What is the same about the shapes you can see? What is different? Are any of the shapes the same? Does it matter about size?*
- *Which of the shapes can roll? Are they all curved? Which shape does not roll?*
- *Which of the shapes can stack? Are they all flat? Which shape does not stack?*

STRENGTHEN Children can try to roll and stack real 3D shapes shown in the **Challenge**. Encourage children to sort the shapes into groups as they test them to see if they are left with an odd one out.

DEEPEN Extend thinking in this **Challenge** by asking children: *Can you find more than one shape that could be the odd one out? Can you give different reasons why the shape might be the odd one out?*

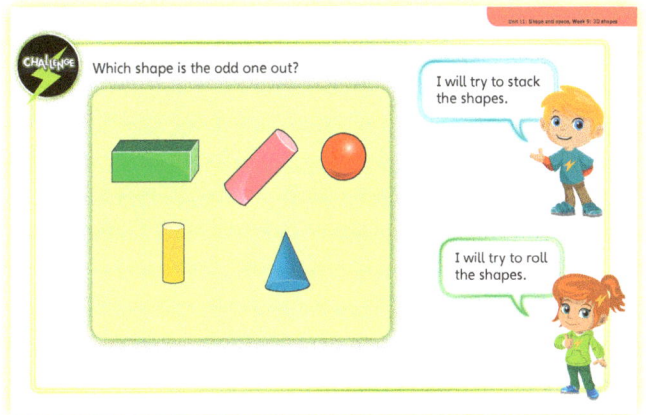

GET ACTIVE Give children a box or a bag and ask them to collect five objects from the classroom, making sure that one of the objects is the 'odd one out'. Their partner has to work out which is the odd one out and explain why.

88

Unit 11: Shape and space, Week 9: 3D shapes

Day 5

Learning focus
Reflecting on the properties of 3D shapes and applying sorting rules

Practical activities

WAYS OF WORKING Whole class

IN FOCUS Children reflect on their understanding of 3D shapes so far this week, focusing on the properties they can describe.

GET ACTIVE **Mystery shapes**
Fill a feely bag with a variety of common 3D shapes. Ask children to put their hand in and feel the shape inside. Can they describe the shapes? Prompt children by asking: *Is it curved or not curved? Does it have any flat faces? How many?* Can children guess what the shape might be? Provide 2D representations of 3D shapes (photocopiable 14) stuck to separate sorting boxes. Ask children to place the shapes from the feely bag into the corresponding sorting box, to prompt their thinking.

Building towers
Use blocks or boxes to build towers. Ask: *Which shape will you choose to start the tower? Why? Who can make the tallest tower?*

Reflect: Journal 2

WAYS OF WORKING Independent thinking

IN FOCUS Children build a tower using four different 3D shapes. At least one of the shapes must roll. Ask children to circle the shapes they have used in their tower and to use their journals to draw their model. Help children with this where necessary. Can children build towers using other sorting rules?

MASTERY CHECKPOINT **Children who have mastered this concept** can build, describe and sort common 3D shapes (sphere, cylinder, cone, cube, cuboid).

Children who have not yet mastered this concept may be able to build, describe and sort some of the common 3D shapes.

Children who have mastered this concept with greater depth can build, describe, sort and compare all 3D shapes (sphere, cylinder, cone, cube, cuboid). They can explain the similarities and differences between the shapes.

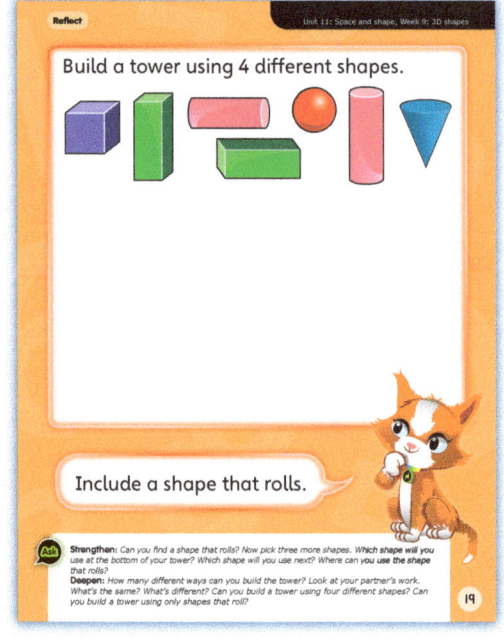

Unit 11: Shape and space, Week 10: 2D shapes

2D shapes

Learning focus
This week, children are introduced to the names of 2D shapes and some of the words to describe their properties. Children will see common 2D shapes shown in different orientations and be encouraged to look for examples of 2D shapes in the world around them.

Small steps
→ Previous step: 3D shapes
→ **This step: 2D shapes**
→ Next step: Making simple patterns

COMMON MISCONCEPTIONS
Children may not be able to identify shapes correctly when they are rotated. Ensure children are given access to images of 2D shapes in a variety of orientations. Ask:
- *If you turn the shape around, can you see what it is now? Is this the same shape as this one? How do you know?*

KEY LANGUAGE
In lesson: square, rectangle, circle, triangle, straight, round, curved, corners, odd one out, same, different

Other language to be used by the teacher: sides, properties, characteristics, roll

RESOURCES
Mandatory: paint, potatoes, 3D shapes, 2D shapes, pictures of 2D shapes, including shapes in the everyday environment (photocopiables 15 and 16)

Optional: chalk, sand or foam, tools for mark marking, paper, playdough, camera, drawing materials, lolly sticks or string

EXPLORE
Taking every opportunity throughout the school day to build and reinforce mathematical concepts gives children's learning purpose and meaning in the wider context of their lives.

ACTIVITY	AREA	DESCRIPTION	RESOURCES
Shape shifter	Art or sand area	Use different tools to draw shapes in sand or foam. Ask: *What shapes can you make? Can you draw straight lines? Can you draw curved lines?*	Sand or foam, tools for mark making
2D prints	Art area	Children make prints from the different faces of 3D shapes. They explore how many different prints can be made from one shape.	Solid 3D shapes, paint, paper
Shape detective	Whole classroom	Challenge children to hunt around the classroom for different shapes. They can either photograph or draw them to show what they have found.	Camera, drawing materials
Potato printing	Art area	Carve potatoes to enable children to print different 2D shapes.	Potatoes, paint, paper

Unit 11: Shape and space, Week 10: 2D shapes

Day 1

Learning focus
Exploring properties of everyday shapes

Before you teach
- How will you encourage children to use correct mathematical vocabulary to describe 2D shapes?
- How will you use your classroom and everyday objects to help children spot 2D shapes?

Starter

PREREQUISITE CHECK

PREREQUISITE CHECK Counting spots shown on a bag and beginning to identify 2D shapes.

WAYS OF WORKING Whole class

IN FOCUS The **Prerequisite check** allows teachers to see if children have retained their counting and number bonds to 10 skills. The picture of the bag is made up from two of the shapes they will be looking at this week. Children may recognise that the bag is a square shape. Encourage children to say the number bond they can see.

ASK
- How many yellow spots are on the bag? How many red spots are on the bag?
- How many spots are there altogether? How do you know?
- What shape is the bag?
- What shapes are the spots?

Shape hunt
We're going on a shape hunt to find some shapes today.
We're going on a shape hunt and this is what we say:
Circles and triangles, where are you?
Squares and rectangles, we need you, too!
Curved sides, straight sides, I wonder what we'll see.
We're going to find some shapes today, I wonder what they'll be!

STIMULUS

STIMULUS Song: Shape hunt

WAYS OF WORKING Whole class

IN FOCUS The song should be played to stimulate interest in 2D shapes. It introduces children to the names of 2D shapes and some of the important vocabulary used to describe them.

ASK
- Which shape names did you hear in the song?
- Did you hear any other special words? [curved, straight]
- Can you see any of these shapes in the classroom?
- What shape is the clock? What shape is the table? What shape is the whiteboard?

GET ACTIVE While singing the song, take children on a shape hunt. As you sing the names in the song, point at the relevant shape in the classroom. You may have to set up or identify a triangular shape beforehand (such as apex of home corner house or a flag).

Unit 11: Shape and space, Week 10: 2D shapes

Day 2

Learning focus
Naming 2D shapes

Discover

WAYS OF WORKING Whole class or small groups
Have 2D shapes available for children to use today. You can use the **2D shape teaching tool** to take a close look at some of the shapes.

IN FOCUS The focus of this **Discover** is for children to begin to recognise common 2D shapes (circle, square, rectangle and triangle) and to describe them using some of the key mathematical language relating to the properties of those shapes.

ASK
- *How many shapes have been printed? Are they all the same?*
- *Can you name any of these shapes?*
- *Can you see any other shapes in the picture?*
- *Can you see any of these shapes in the classroom?*

STRENGTHEN Give children the chance to print their own 2D shapes and look at how they match the ones in the picture.

DEEPEN Encourage children to identify shapes from the picture in the classroom. Ask: *How many of each shape can you find? What can you find the most of? What can you find the least of?*

Share

WAYS OF WORKING Whole class

IN FOCUS Children are introduced to the names of common 2D shapes: circle, triangle, rectangle, square, and are encouraged to describe some of their properties. Children compare what is the same and what is different about the shapes, using the terms *sides, corners, straight, curved*.

ASK
- *Can you point to the circle? Can you point to the square?*
- *How many sides does the triangle have? How many corners does the rectangle have?*
- *What is the same or different about the square and the rectangle?*
- *Which shapes have straight sides? Which shape has curved sides?*
- *Can you draw a rectangle in the air with your finger? Are you drawing curved or straight lines?*

STRENGTHEN Encourage children to draw straight and curved lines in the air with their fingers. Ask children to make straight and curved lines with different parts of their bodies. Familiarity with the vocabulary *curved* and *straight* is the focus of this activity.

DEEPEN Encourage children to use the shape names and properties by playing a game of 'I spy'. Children choose a

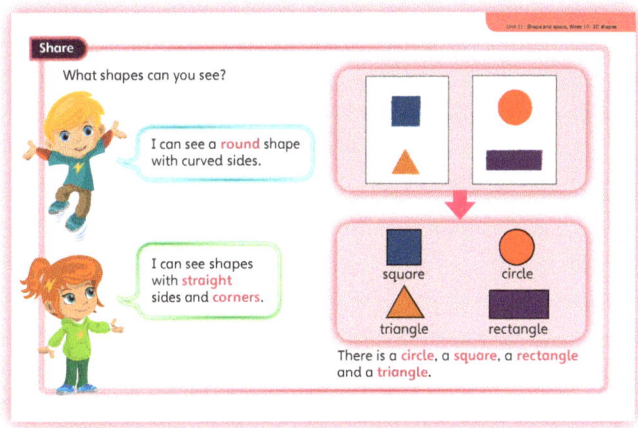

shape they can see in the classroom and challenge other children to guess the shape by using one property to describe it, for example: *I spy with my little eye, a shape that has a curved side.*

GET ACTIVE Draw large-scale shapes in the playground using chalk. Show the shape cards (photocopiable 15) one at a time. Children should stand inside the matching shape. Repeat saying the names of the 2D shapes. Can children recognise the names and stand inside the correct shape?

Unit 11: Shape and space, Week 10: 2D shapes

Day 3

Learning focus

Identifying 2D shapes and describing similarities and differences

Think together

WAYS OF WORKING Whole class

Ensure 2D shapes in a variety of orientations are available for children to look at today.

IN FOCUS The aim of Question ❶ is for children to practise identifying shapes, this time in different contexts. They should look for the circles, but may also identify other shapes in the picture. Question ❷ asks children to identify the odd one out from a set shapes made up of rectangles shown in different orientations and one right-angled triangle. This helps children to see that shapes are still the same even when they are rotated. Use the **2D shapes teaching tool** to rotate shapes to demonstrate this. Asking what is the same about the shapes helps children to see the similarities between them.

ASK

- Question ❶: *How many circles can you see? Do they have curved or straight sides? Can you see any other shapes?*
- Question ❷: *What is the same about the shapes? Which of the shapes are the same? Can you name any of the shapes? Is it still a rectangle if we turn it around?*
- Question ❷: *What is the name of the shape that is the odd one out? How is it different from the other shapes?*

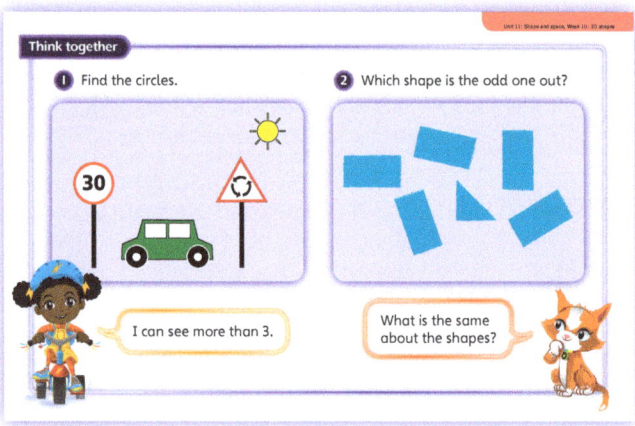

STRENGTHEN Use a selection of 2D shape flashcards (photocopiable 15), including representations of 2D shapes that children will see everyday (photocopiable 16). Play a memory game with up to 12 cards on the table. Children turn two cards over at a time, and if the shapes match they keep the cards. Encourage children to say the name of the shapes they collect.

DEEPEN Use a selection of 2D shape flashcards, as in **Strengthen**. Play shape snap. When children see two shapes that are the same they shout 'snap' plus the name of the shape, for example: *Snap: triangle.*

Practice: Journal 1

WAYS OF WORKING Independent thinking

IN FOCUS Children identify 2D shapes shown in different sizes and orientations. They identify the triangles in a beach scene and find the rectangle as the odd one out in a set with three squares, in different proportions and orientations. Discuss the similarities and differences between the shapes they see, considering their size and the number of sides.

MASTERY CHECKPOINT Children can name 2D shapes and describe some of their characteristics.

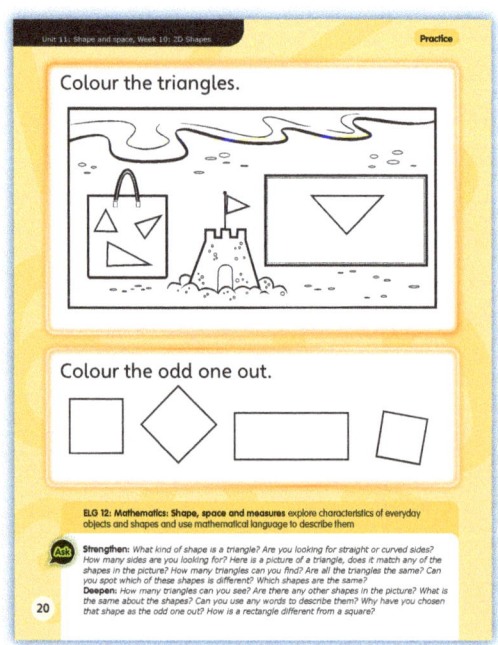

93

Unit 11: Shape and space, Week 10: 2D shapes

Day 4

Learning focus
Identifying 2D shapes within 3D shapes

Challenge

WAYS OF WORKING Whole class or in pairs
Ensure you have a selection of 3D shapes available to touch and possibly print with. Use the **3D shapes teaching tool** to rotate the solid shapes so that children can see all the faces.

IN FOCUS Children recap 3D shapes and use them to print 2D shapes. They consider the different 2D shapes on the faces of 3D objects. Children see that different 3D shapes can still make the same 2D print.

ASK
- Which solid shapes can you see? What shape is the print?
- What shape print do you think the cylinder will make? What shape print do you think the cube will make?
- Which shapes would print a circle? Which shapes would print a square?
- How many different prints will the rectangle make?
- Can you make a print from the curved part of a shape?

STRENGTHEN Give children a range of 3D shapes and some paint to print with, or some playdough to press the shapes into. They explore what shapes the different surfaces of the 3D shapes make.

DEEPEN Children use a range of 3D shapes to print a picture. The shapes can overlap, but should still be identifiable.

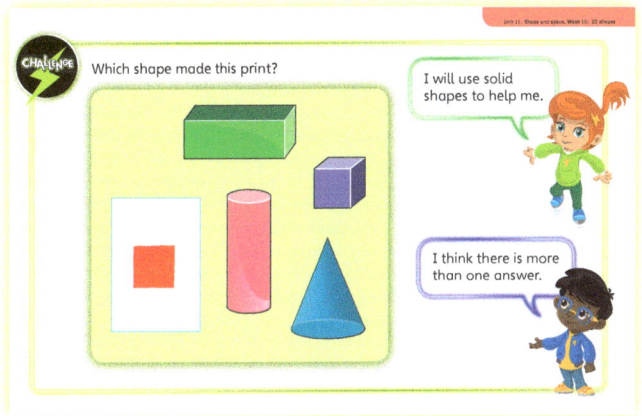

GET ACTIVE Ask children to create a picture by printing a selection of 2D shapes from the faces of 3D shapes, so that some prints are overlapping (see **Deepen**). They then work with a partner to compare their pictures and describe each other's shapes. Children try to work out which 3D shapes their partner used to make the picture. Ask: *What shapes can you see? Which solid shapes could have made these prints?*

Unit 11: Shape and space, Week 10: 2D shapes

Day 5

Learning focus
Identifying 2D shapes in different contexts

Practical activities

WAYS OF WORKING Whole class

IN FOCUS The focus of these **Practical activities** is to recap the names of the 2D shapes, prompting children to discuss their properties and characteristics as they carry them out. Draw children's attention particularly to the everyday representations of common 2D shapes they see in their environment.

GET ACTIVE Corners
Place images of a square, rectangle, circle and triangle in real life contexts (enlarged photocopiable 16) in different parts of the room or outside area. Show children a picture of a standard 2D shape. They run to the corner where that shape is.

Making shapes
Children use lolly sticks or string to make circles, rectangles, squares and triangles. Encourage children to trace the outline of 2D shapes then draw them. Can they then make or draw their own 2D shapes? Ask: *Which shape cannot be made from sticks? Why? Is it easier to make the rectangle with sticks or with string?* Encourage children to think about the straight and curved sides of the shapes.

Human shapes
Ask children to work in small groups and make the shapes that you call out using only their bodies. Can they stand in a circle? Can they stand in a triangle? Do they need to make straight or curved lines?

Shape hunt
Children go on a shape hunt around the classroom or outside area. Challenge them to find three circles, or as many squares as they can. Children can sing the song from the **Stimulus** as they hunt.

Reflect: Journal 2

WAYS OF WORKING Independent thinking

IN FOCUS Children match 3D shapes to their corresponding 2D prints.

MASTERY CHECKPOINT **Children who have mastered this concept** can match 3D shapes to their 2D prints and name each 2D shape.

Children who have not yet mastered this concept can see 2D shapes on 3D objects and start to describe the shapes they see, including using the shape names.

Children who have mastered this concept with greater depth can match 3D shapes to their prints and highlight which 3D shapes have more than one print. They can describe the prints they make using the shape names.

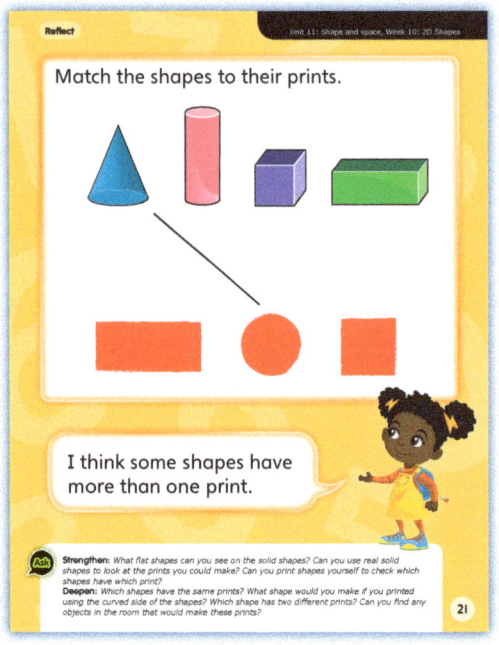

95

Power Maths Reception Observation Sheet

Unit 6 – Numbers bonds within 5

Date:

Adult observing:

Children observed

Unit objective(s)

Exploring number bonds within 5 using the part-whole model
- Sorting objects into two groups
- Sorting a whole into two distinct parts
- Recognising different representations of two parts
- Finding different ways to sort groups into parts
- Finding number bonds to 3, 4 and 5

What did you observe?

Try to include details such as: What prompted the behaviour? What did the children do? What did they say to you or to others? How did you (or others) respond?

Was this activity:
- ☐ Independent
- ☐ Guided
- ☐ Directed

What are your next steps to help these children deepen their understanding of the concept?

© Pearson Education Ltd 2019. This page may be photocopied for use within the purchasing organisation.

Power Maths Reception Observation Sheet

Unit 7 – Numbers to 10

Date:

Adult observing:

Children observed

Unit objective(s)

Counting to 10
- Counting to 6, 7, 8, 9 and 10
- Cardinality of numbers to 10
- Counting different representations up to 10
- Representations of numbers to 10
- Counting using abstraction
- Counting up to 10 from a larger group

What did you observe?

Try to include details such as: What prompted the behaviour? What did the children do? What did they say to you or to others? How did you (or others) respond?

Was this activity:
- ☐ Independent
- ☐ Guided
- ☐ Directed

What are your next steps to help these children deepen their understanding of the concept?

© Pearson Education Ltd 2019. This page may be photocopied for use within the purchasing organisation.

Power Maths Reception Observation Sheet

Unit 8 – Comparing numbers within 10

Date:

Adult observing:

Children observed

Unit objective(s)

Comparing groups up to 10
- Compare groups up to 10
- Compare and represent numbers to 10
- More than and fewer than
- How many more?
- Finding the difference

What did you observe?

Try to include details such as: What prompted the behaviour? What did the children do? What did they say to you or to others? How did you (or others) respond?

Was this activity:
☐ Independent
☐ Guided
☐ Directed

What are your next steps to help these children deepen their understanding of the concept?

© Pearson Education Ltd 2019. This page may be photocopied for use within the purchasing organisation.

Power Maths Reception Observation Sheet

Unit 9 – Addition to 10

Date:

Adult observing:

Children observed

Unit objective(s)
Combining 2 groups to find the whole
- Recapping the language of parts and wholes
- Combining 2 parts to make a whole
- Exploring the part-whole model
- Exploring misconceptions using the part-whole model
- Number stories to 10 using the part-whole model

What did you observe?

Try to include details such as: What prompted the behaviour? What did the children do? What did they say to you or to others? How did you (or others) respond?

Was this activity:
☐ Independent
☐ Guided
☐ Directed

What are your next steps to help these children deepen their understanding of the concept?

© Pearson Education Ltd 2019. This page may be photocopied for use within the purchasing organisation.

Power Maths Reception Observation Sheet

Unit 10 – Number bonds to 10

Date:

Adult observing:

Children observed

Unit objective(s)
Number bonds to 10
- Exploring the composition of 10
- Using knowledge of number bonds to 10 to work out how many more
- Consolidating number bonds to 10
- Using the part-whole model to break 10 into two parts
- Identifying the whole and parts when variation is a factor
- Using number bonds to 10 to break a whole into parts
- Exploring all the number bonds to 10

What did you observe?

Try to include details such as: What prompted the behaviour? What did the children do? What did they say to you or to others? How did you (or others) respond?

Was this activity:
☐ Independent
☐ Guided
☐ Directed

What are your next steps to help these children deepen their understanding of the concept?

© Pearson Education Ltd 2019. This page may be photocopied for use within the purchasing organisation.

Power Maths Reception Observation Sheet

Unit 11 – Shape and space

Date:

Adult observing:

Children observed

Unit objective(s)
Spatial awareness, 2D and 3D shapes
- Understanding and using positional and directional language in practical contexts
- Using directional and positional language to describe a route
- Exploring properties of everyday shapes
- Exploring, describing and comparing the properties of 3D shapes
- Similarities and differences between 3D shapes and applying sorting rules
- Identifying and naming 2D shapes and describing similarities and differences
- Identifying 2D shapes within 3D shapes
- Identifying 2D shapes in the environment

What did you observe?

Try to include details such as: What prompted the behaviour? What did the children do? What did they say to you or to others? How did you (or others) respond?

Was this activity:
☐ Independent
☐ Guided
☐ Directed

What are your next steps to help these children deepen their understanding of the concept?

© Pearson Education Ltd 2019. This page may be photocopied for use within the purchasing organisation.

Photocopiable 1: Number 6

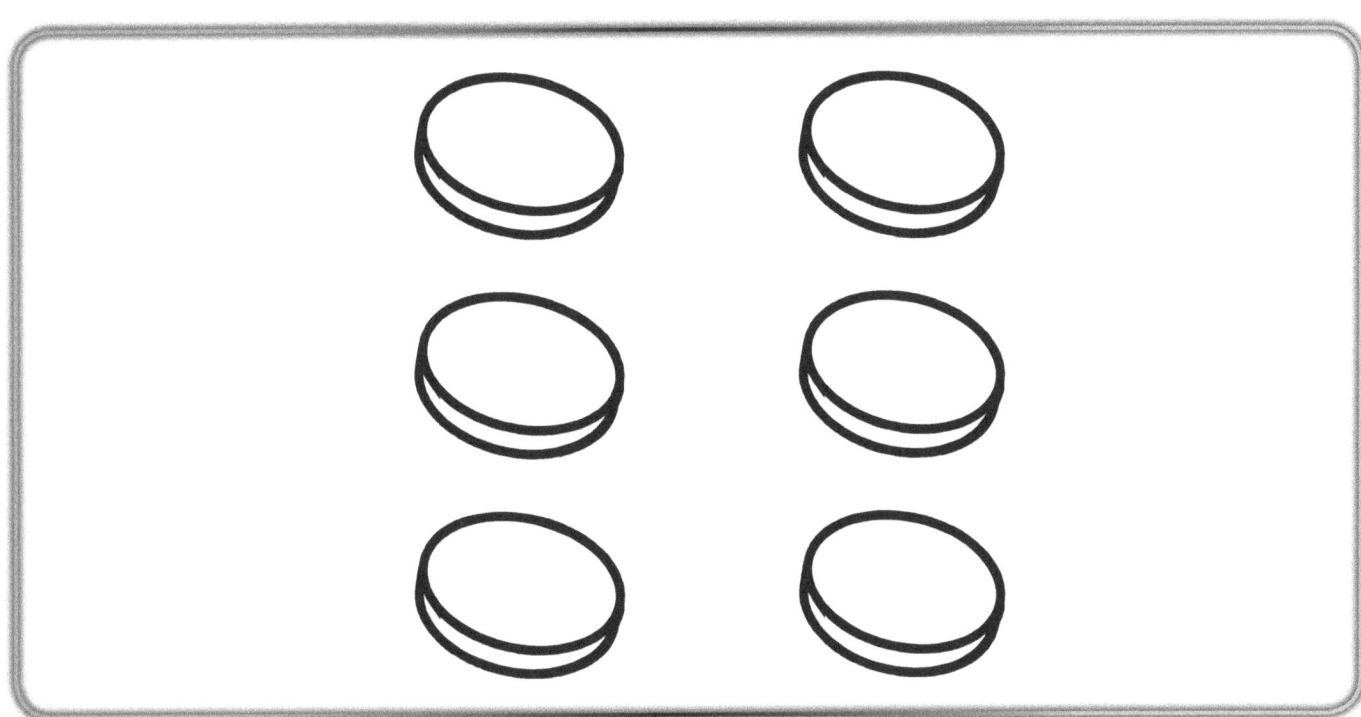

Photocopiable 2: Number 7

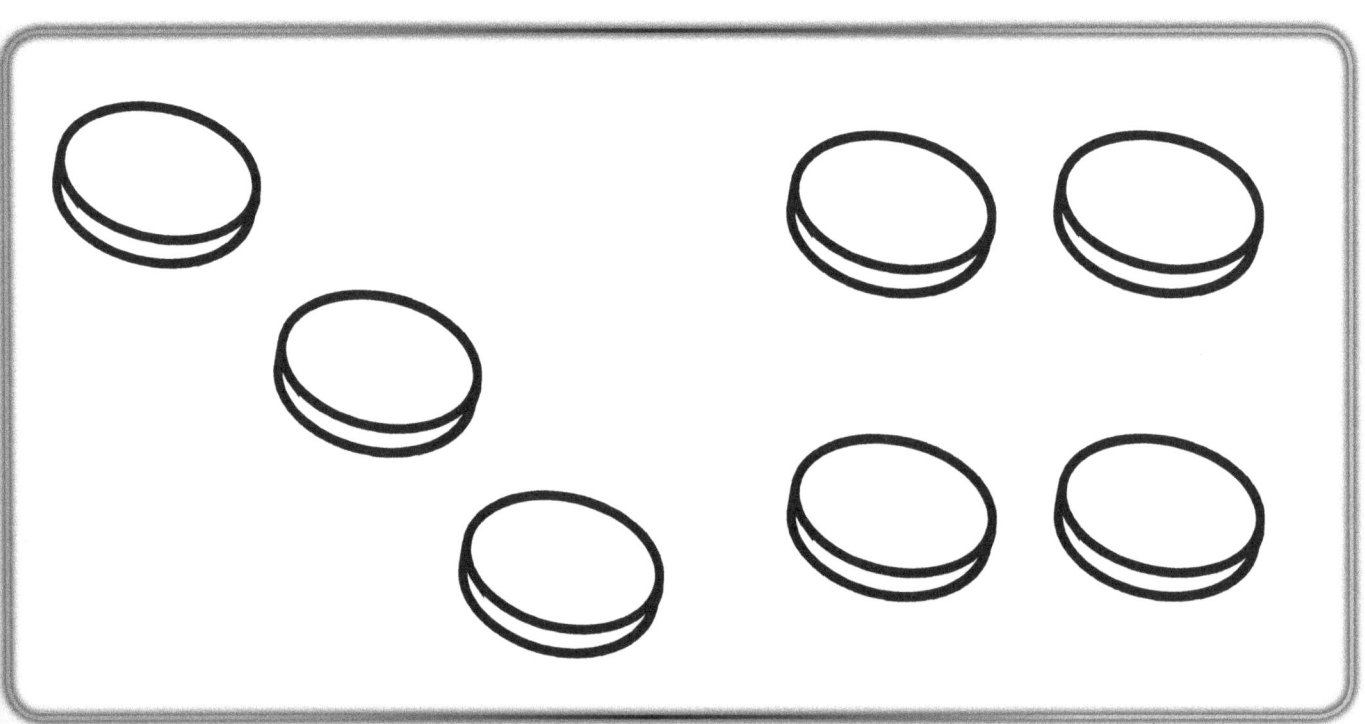

Photocopiable 3: Number 8

Photocopiable 4: Number 9

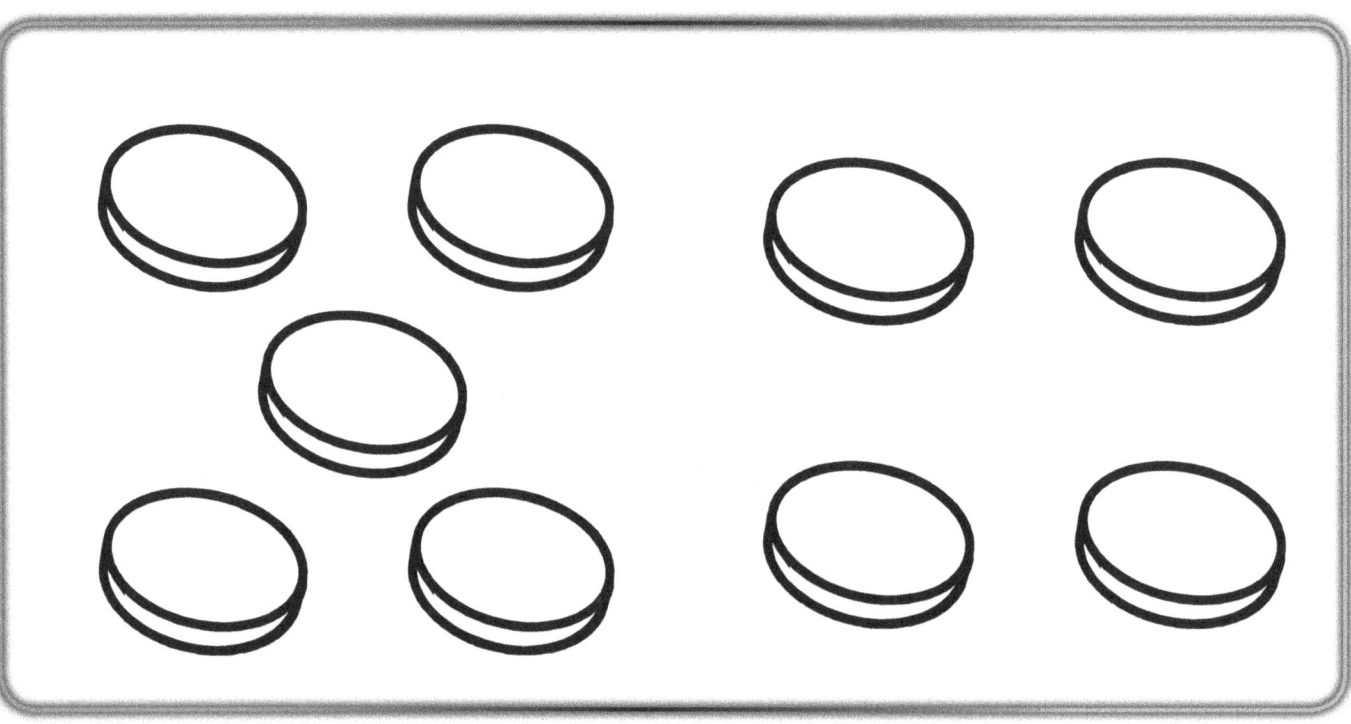

Photocopiable 5: Number 10

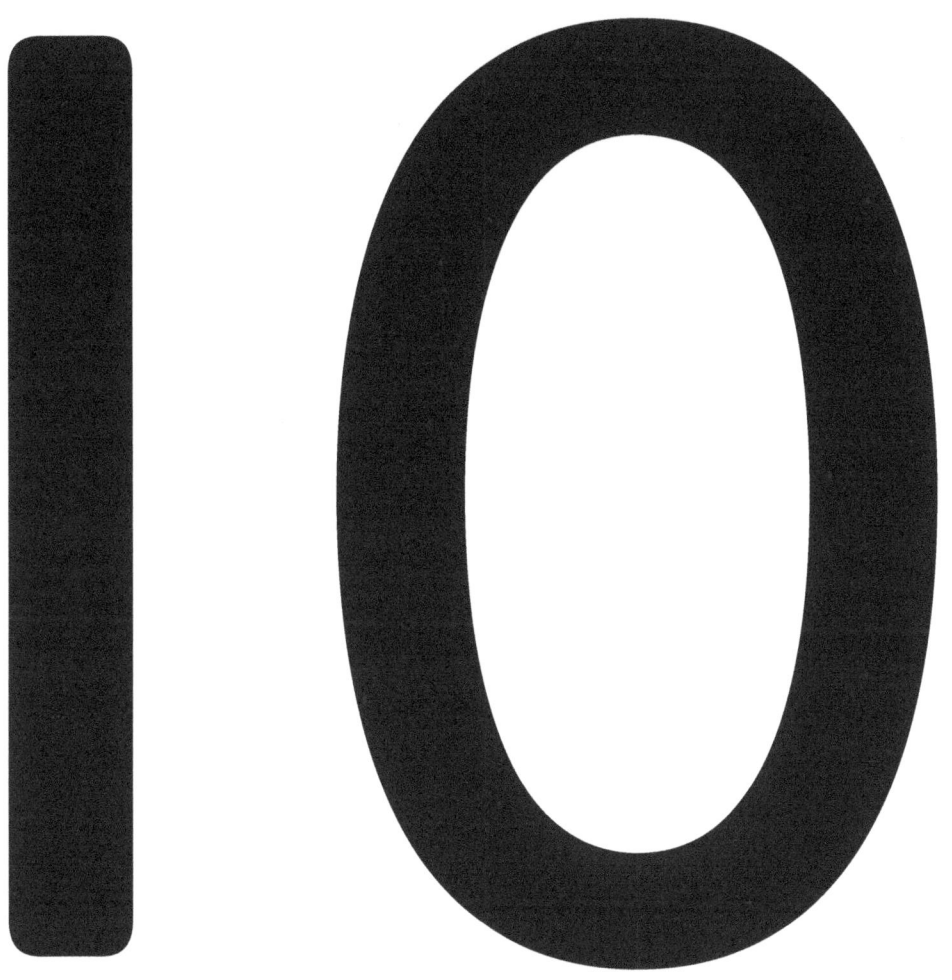

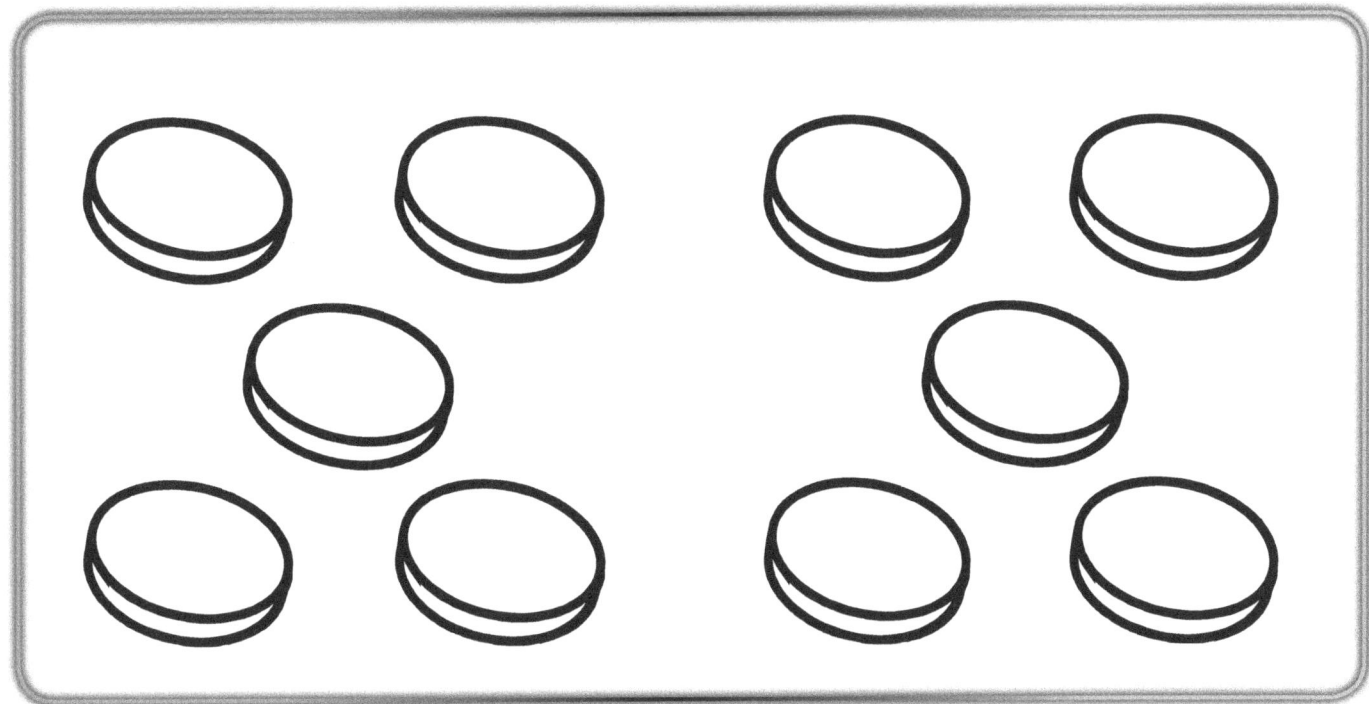

Photocopiable 6: Ten frame

Photocopiable 7: Part-whole model

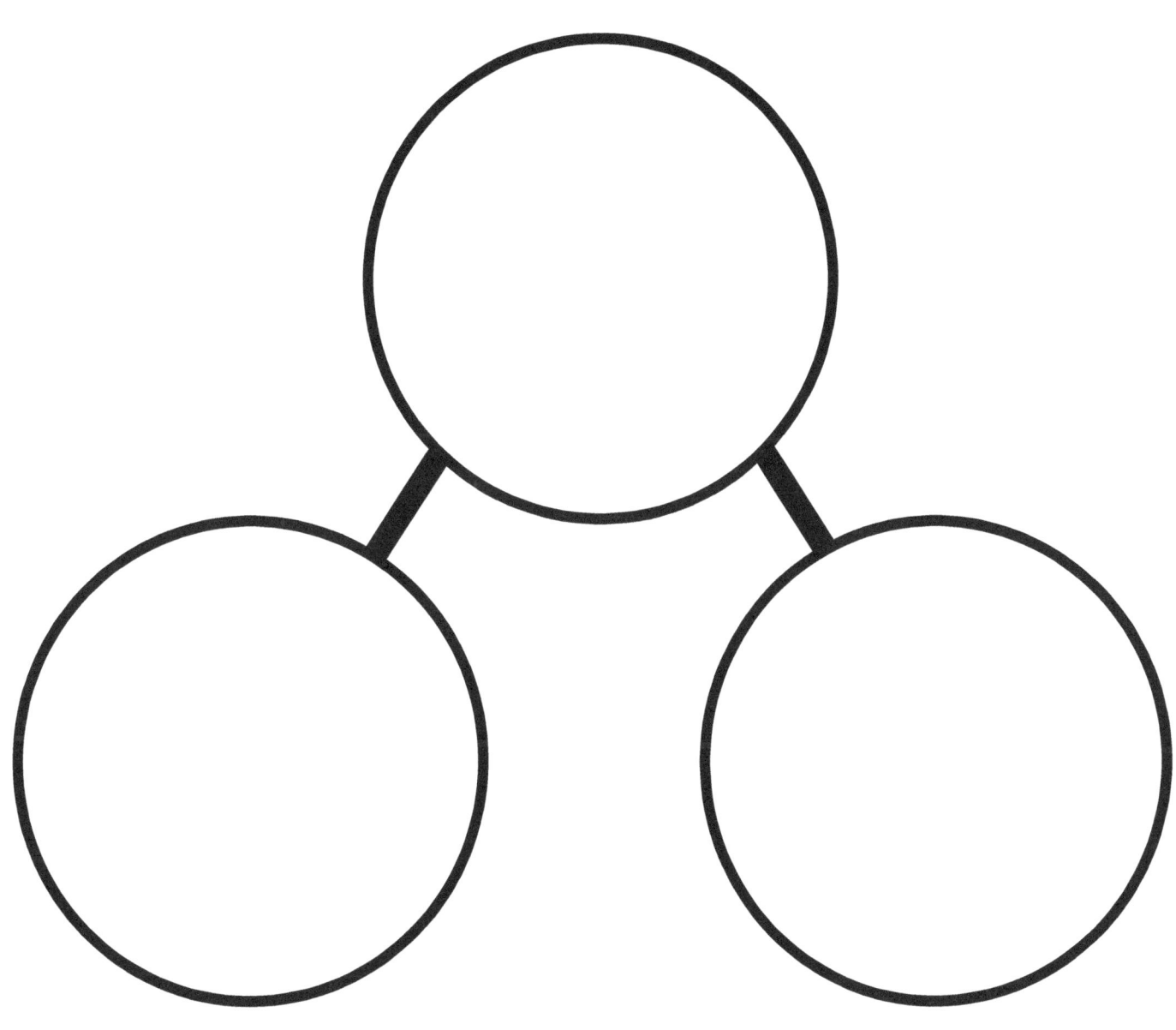

Photocopiable 9: Ladybird template

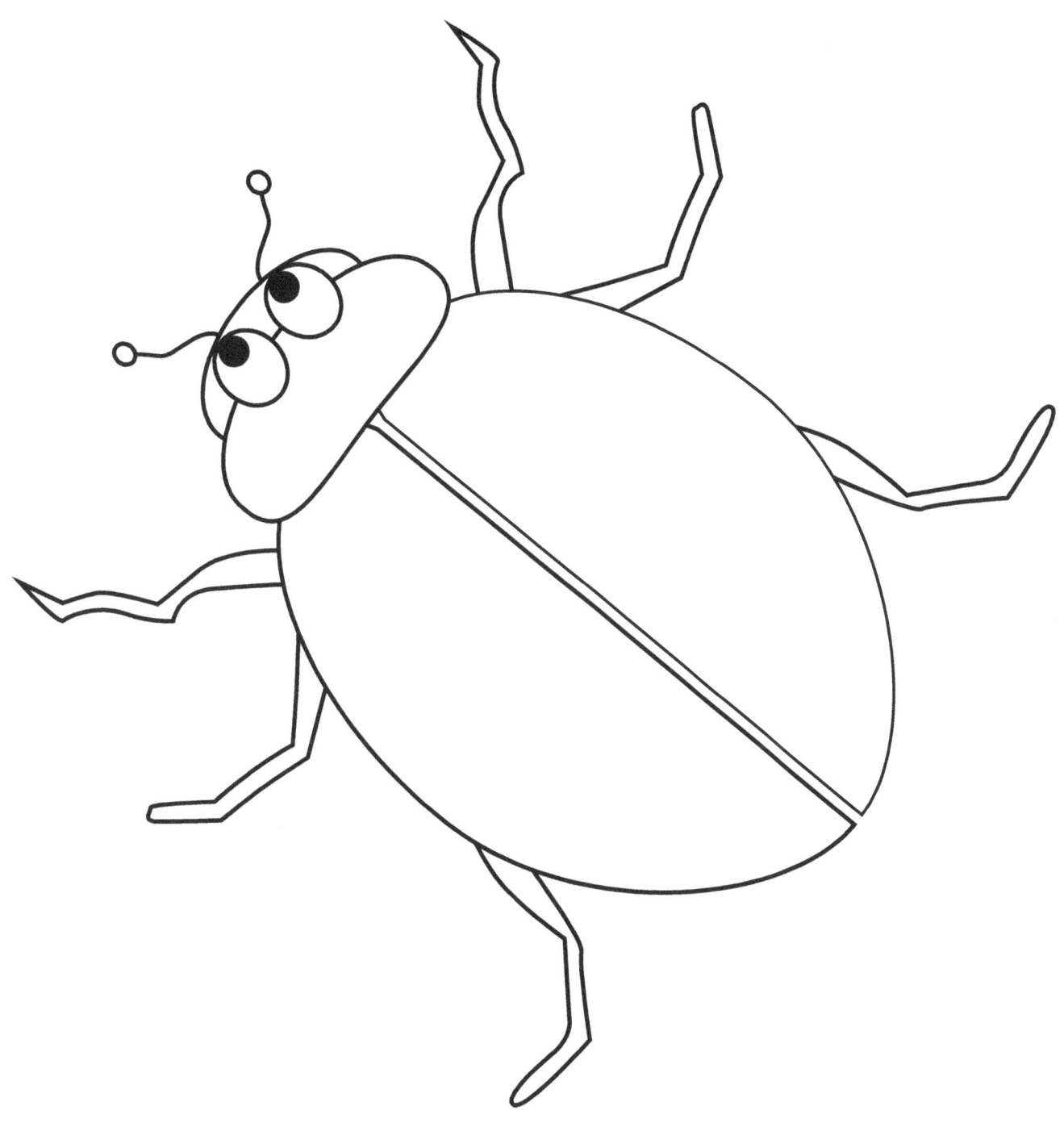

Photocopiable 11: Small part-whole models

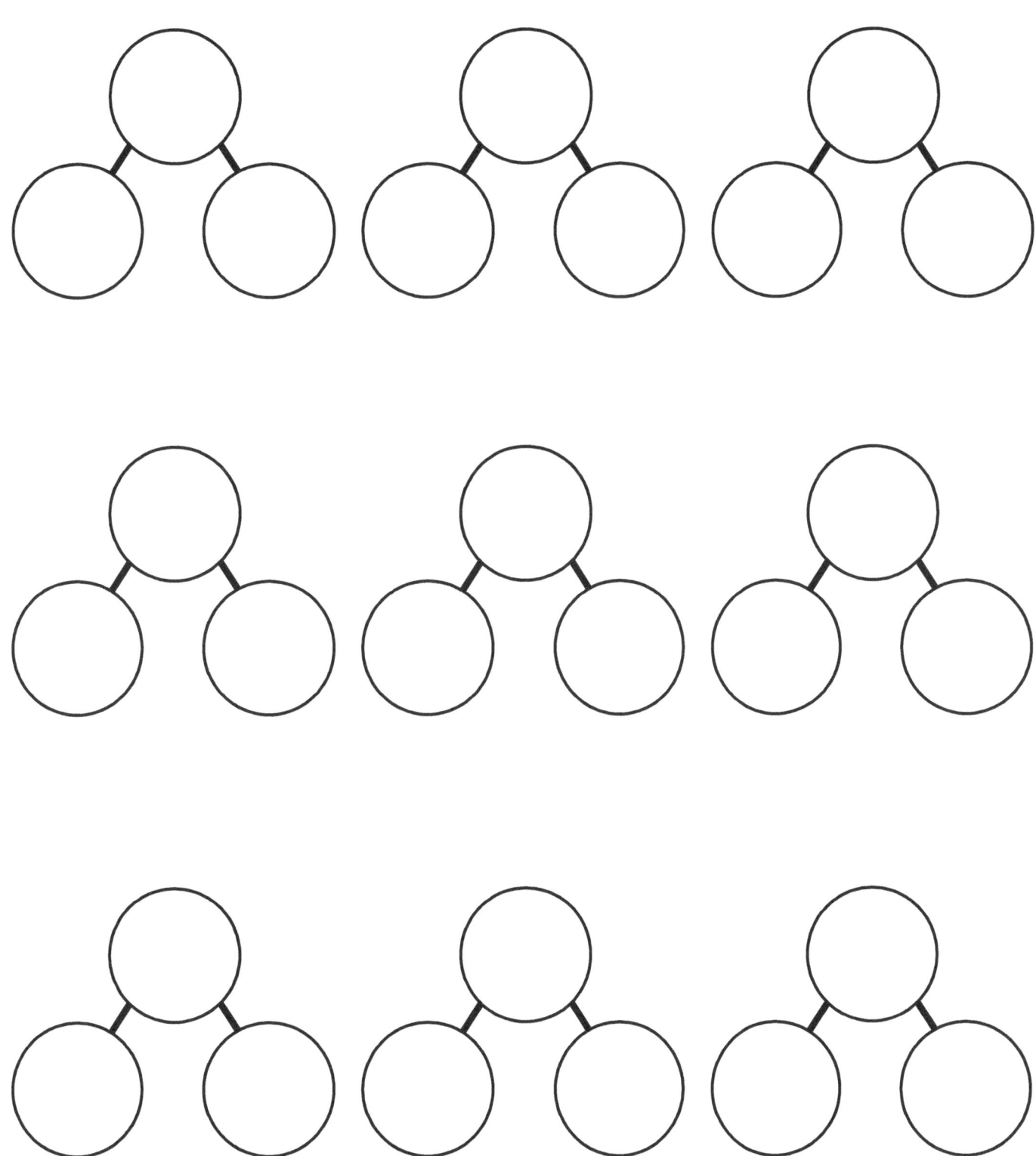

Photocopiable 12: Positional language

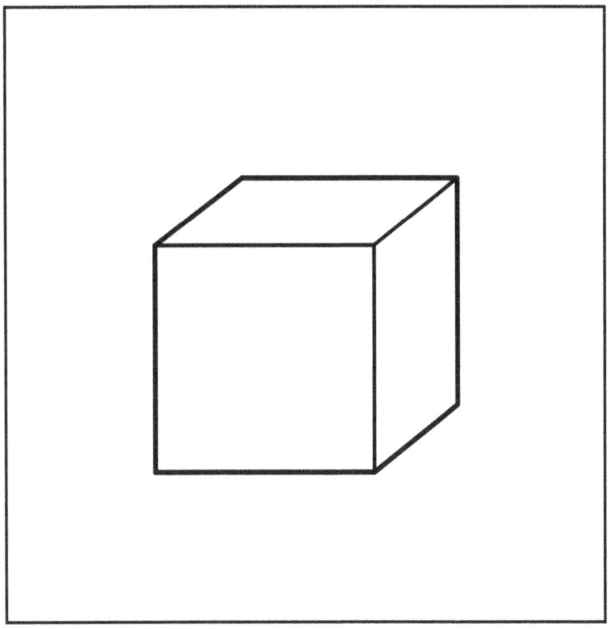

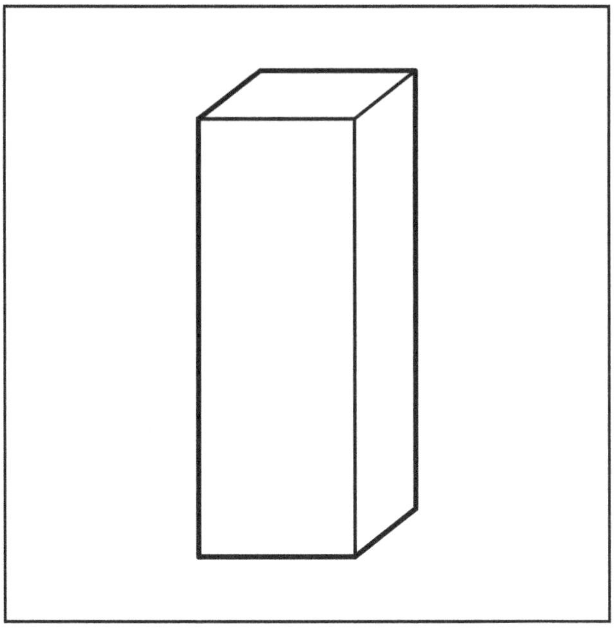

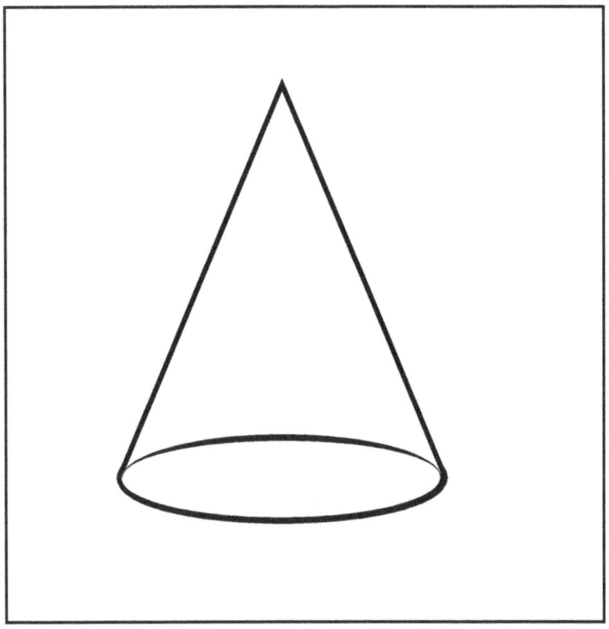

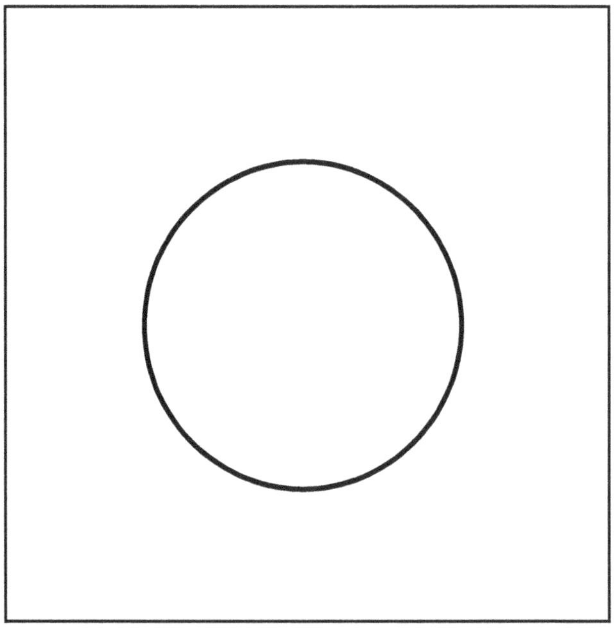

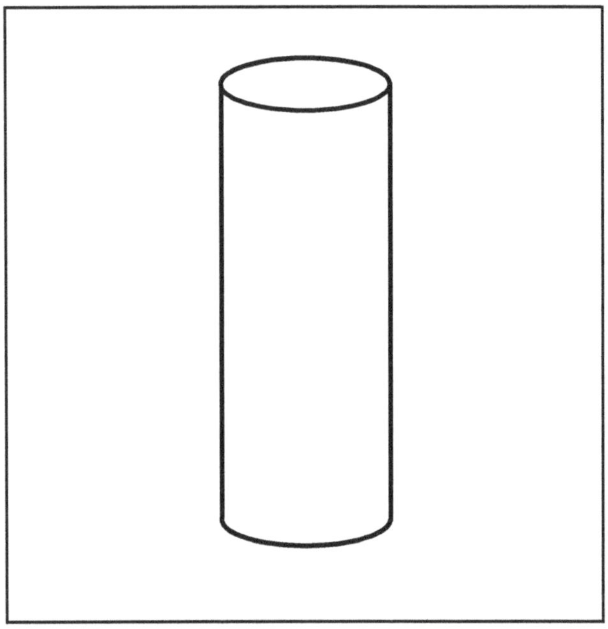

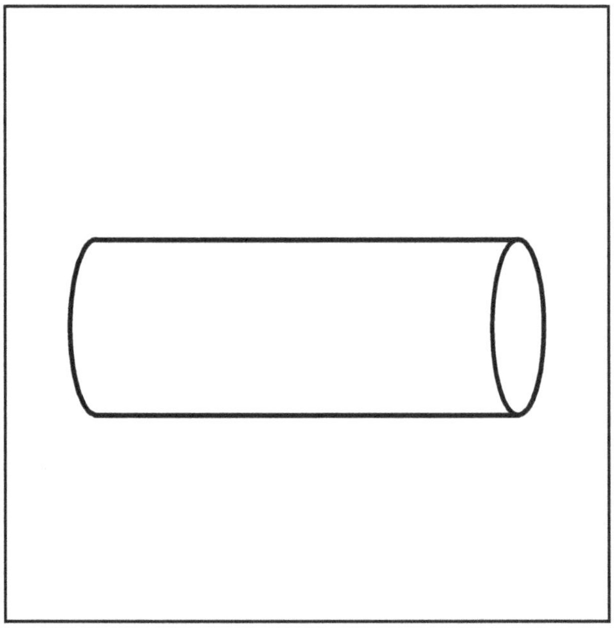

Photocopiable 14: 3D shapes

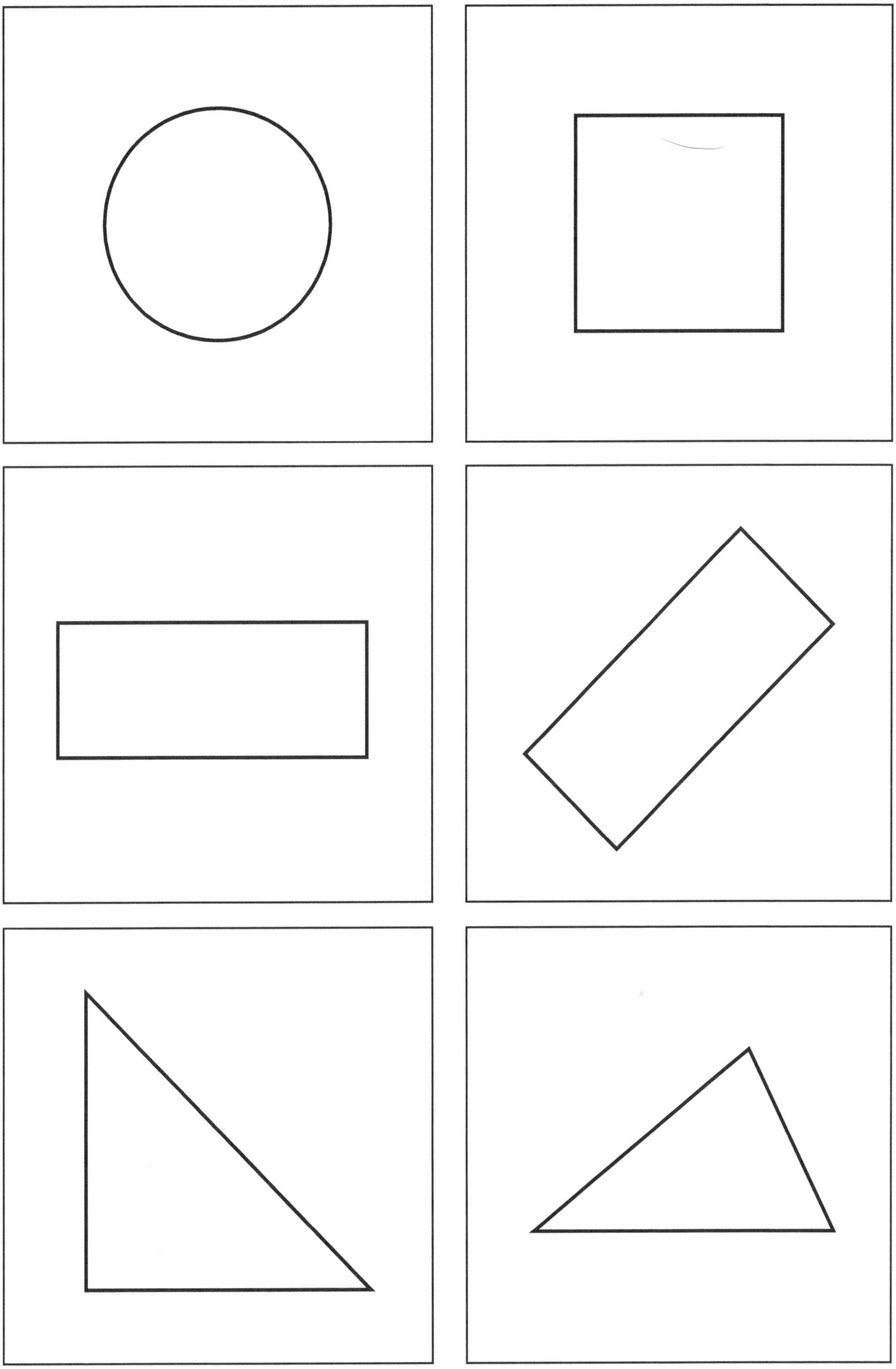

Photocopiable 15: 2D shapes

116

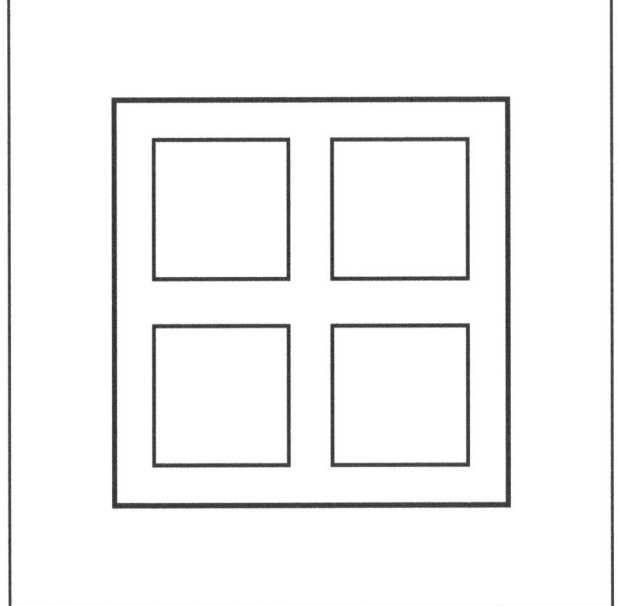

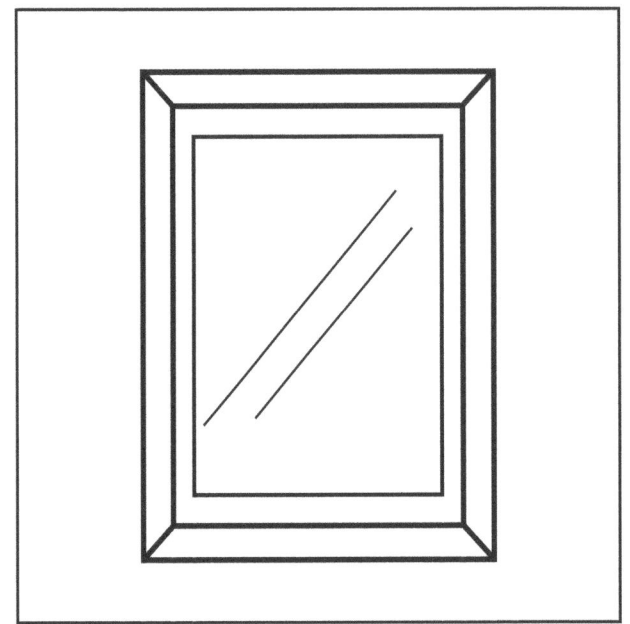

List of practical resources

Reception Term B Mandatory resources

Resource	Lesson
2D shapes	**Unit 11** week 10
3D shapes	**Unit 11** weeks 9, 10
Building blocks	**Unit 11** week 9
Buttons	**Unit 7** week 3
Counters (double-sided or in two colours)	**Unit 7** weeks 2, 3 **Unit 8** week 4 **Unit 9** week 5 **Unit 10** weeks 6, 7
Drinking bottles	**Unit 10** week 6
Empty boxes	**Unit 11** week 9
Hula hoops	**Unit 6** week 1 **Unit 9** week 5
Multilink cubes	**Unit 6** week 1 **Unit 7** weeks 2, 3 **Unit 8** week 4 **Unit 9** week 5 **Unit 10** week 7
Paint	**Unit 11** week 10
Part-whole model (photocopiable 7)	**Unit 9** week 5 **Unit 10** week 7
Pictures of 2D shapes, including shapes in the everyday environment (photocopiables 15 and 16)	**Unit 11** week 10
Potatoes	**Unit 11** week 10
Pots, soil and seedlings	**Unit 9** week 5

Reception Term B Optional resources

Resource	Lesson
2D representations of 3D shapes (photocopiable 14)	**Unit 11** week 9
3D shapes	**Unit 11** week 9
Action cards (photocopiable 10)	**Unit 7** week 3
Balls	**Unit 6** week 1 **Unit 10** week 6 **Unit 11** week 9
Bead strings	**Unit 7** weeks 2, 3 **Unit 10** weeks 6, 7
Bean bags	**Unit 6** week 1 **Unit 7** week 3 **Unit 8** week 4 **Unit 10** week 7 **Unit 11** week 8
Boxes or containers	**Unit 7** weeks 2, 3 **Unit 11** week 8
Building blocks	**Unit 8** week 4
Butterfly template (photocopiable 8)	**Unit 7** week 2
Buttons	**Unit 10** week 7
Camera	**Unit 11** week 10

Resource	Lesson
Candles (in two colours)	**Unit 6** week 1 **Unit 10** week 6
Card	**Unit 7** week 3
Chalk	**Unit 11** weeks 8, 9, 10
Cushions	**Unit 8** week 4
Dice	**Unit 7** week 3
Digit cards (1–10)	**Unit 6** week 1 **Unit 7** week 3 **Unit 8** week 4 **Unit 9** week 5 **Unit 10** weeks 6, 7
Doll's house and furniture, including play people, toy bed, toy car	**Unit 11** week 8
Feely bag	**Unit 11** week 9
Flowers	**Unit 9** week 5
Glue	**Unit 7** week 3 **Unit 10** week 7 **Unit 11** week 8
Home corner items, including paper plates, cups, bowls	**Unit 7** weeks 2, 3 **Unit 8** week 4 **Unit 10** week 7
Hula hoops	**Unit 6** week 1 **Unit 7** week 3 **Unit 8** week 4 **Unit 10** week 7 **Unit 11** week 9
Ladybird template (photocopiable 9)	**Unit 7** week 2 **Unit 10** week 6
Large arrows (photocopiable 13)	**Unit 11** week 8
Large play bricks	**Unit 10** week 6 **Unit 11** weeks 8, 9
Lolly sticks	**Unit 7** week 2 **Unit 11** week 10
Magnifying glass	**Unit 7** week 2
Marbles	**Unit 7** week 2
Outdoor slide or slope	**Unit 11** week 9
Paper shapes	**Unit 10** week 7
PE equipment (bibs, balls, bats, mats, benches, hoops, crawling tubes, cones)	**Unit 8** week 4 **Unit 11** weeks 8, 9
Pencils, paper, pens, and pencil pots	**Unit 6** week 1 **Unit 8** week 4 **Unit 11** weeks 8, 10, 11
Pipe cleaners	**Unit 7** week 2
Pipe-cleaner flowers or pictures of flowers	**Unit 9** week 5
Plant pots and seeds	**Unit 7** week 2
Plastic bottles or skittles or bowling pins	**Unit 6** week 1 **Unit 10** week 6
Playdough	**Unit 6** week 1 **Unit 10** week 6 **Unit 11** weeks 9, 11
Positional language flashcards (photocopiable 12)	**Unit 11** week 8
Precious stones	**Unit 7** week 3
Programmable toy or remote control car	**Unit 11** week 8
Recording equipment	**Unit 11** week 8

Resource	Lesson
Recycled material (paper tubes, boxes, cartons)	**Unit 11** weeks 8, 9
Sand or foam	**Unit 11** week 10
Selection of classroom items, small toys and real-life natural objects for counting and sorting	**Unit 7** weeks 2, 3 **Unit 9** week 5
Shells	**Unit 7** week 3
Small part-whole models (photocopiable 11)	**Unit 10** week 7
Skipping ropes	**Unit 6** week 1
Soft toys or teddies	**Unit 8** week 4 **Unit 11** week 8
Stickers	**Unit 8** week 4
Stick-on eyes and sticky spots in different colours	**Unit 7** week 2
Sticky tape	**Unit 11** week 8
Ten frame (photocopiable 6)	**Unit 8** week 4
Tin	**Unit 7** week 2
Tissue paper	**Unit 9** week 5
Tools for mark making	**Unit 11** week 10
Toy animals or pictures of animals	**Unit 8** week 4
Toy fish	**Unit 10** week 7

Power Maths Reception, yearly overview

Spring term

Strand	Unit		Week	Weekly title	Early Learning Goal
Number – addition and subtraction	Unit 6	Number bonds within 5	1	Introducing the part-whole model	Pre-requisite to: Using quantities and objects, they add and subtract 2 single-digit numbers and count on or back to find the answer.
Number – number and place value	Unit 7	Numbers to 10	2	Counting to 6, 7 and 8	Children count reliably with numbers from 1 to 20, place them in order.
			3	Counting to 9 and 10	
Number – number and place value	Unit 8	Comparing numbers within 10	4	Comparing groups up to 10	Children explore characteristics of everyday objects.
Number – addition and subtraction	Unit 9	Addition to 10	5	Combining 2 groups to find the whole	Using quantities and objects, they add and subtract 2 single-digit numbers and count on or back to find the answer.
Number – addition and subtraction	Unit 10	Number bonds to 10	6	Using a ten frame	Pre-requisite to: Using quantities and objects, they add and subtract 2 single-digit numbers and count on or back to find the answer.
			7	The part-whole model to 10	
Geometry – properties of shape	Unit 11	Shape and space	8	Spacial awareness	Children explore characteristics of everyday objects and shapes and use mathematical language to describe them.
			9	3D shapes	
			10	2D shapes	

Power Maths Reception, yearly overview

Autumn term

Strand	Unit		Week	Weekly title	Early Learning Goal
Number – number and place value	Unit 1	Numbers to 5	1	Counting to 1, 2 and 3	Children count reliably with numbers from 1 to 20, place them in order.
			2	Counting to 4	
			3	Counting to 5	
Number – addition and subtraction	Unit 2	Sorting	4	Sorting into 2 groups	Children explore characteristics of everyday objects.
Number – number and place value	Unit 3	Comparing groups within 5	5	Comparing quantities of identical objects	Pre-requisite to: Using quantities and objects, they add and subtract 2 single-digit numbers and count on or back to find the answer.
			6	Comparing quantities of non-identical objects	
Number – addition and subtraction	Unit 4	Change within 5	7	One more	Say which number is one more or one less than a given number.
			8	One less	
Measurement	Unit 5	Time	9	My day	Children use everyday language to talk about time to solve problems.

Your *Power Maths Reception* resources

Teacher Guides

Think of your **Teacher Guides** as *Power Maths* handbooks that will guide, support and inspire your day-to-day teaching. Clear and concise, and illustrated with helpful examples, your **Teacher Guides** will help you make the best possible use of every individual lesson. They also provide wrap-around professional development, enhancing your own subject knowledge and helping you to grow in confidence about moving your children forward together.

There is a **Teacher Guide** for every term with unit, weekly and lesson level guidance and support.

Helpful guidance on teaching for mastery, managing the lesson sequence and getting the best from the lesson resources.

Annotations for every **Online Flashcard** and **Maths Journal** page, providing prompts for key questions to ask to expose understanding and explanations as to why key questions have been chosen.

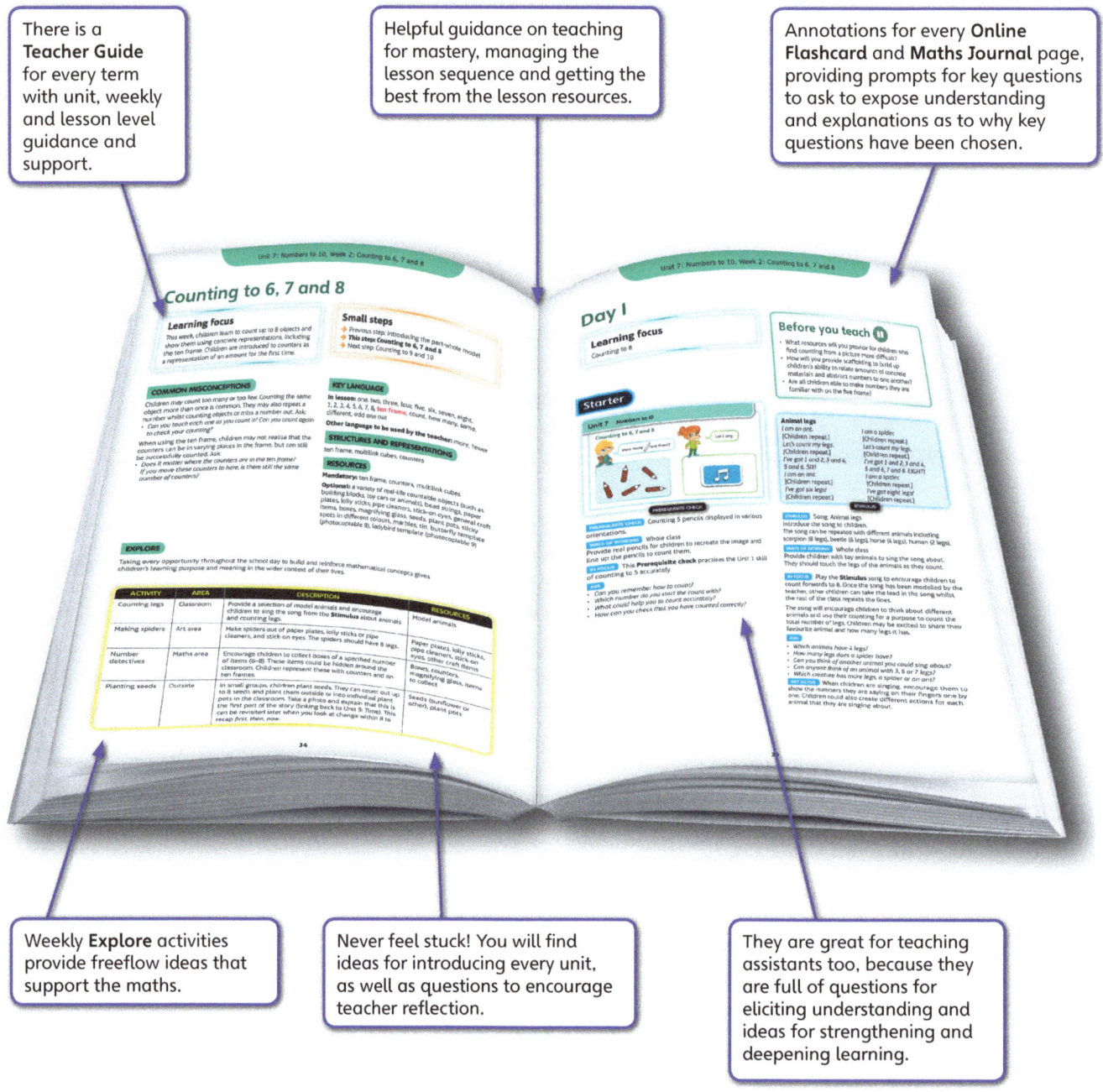

Weekly **Explore** activities provide freeflow ideas that support the maths.

Never feel stuck! You will find ideas for introducing every unit, as well as questions to encourage teacher reflection.

They are great for teaching assistants too, because they are full of questions for eliciting understanding and ideas for strengthening and deepening learning.

Your *Power Maths Reception* resources

Maths Journals

The **Maths Journals** have been designed to support best practice in Early Years, whilst also providing evidence that each child has mastered a concept.

The journal activities can be guided or child-initiated, depending on your school's ethos.

Children are encouraged to choose how they demonstrate their understanding of the concept – those who are ready might write or draw their answers, but equally they may choose to place concrete objects on the page and move them around to demonstrate their understanding if they prefer. Any representation is fine, as long as it shows that they have understood the mathematical concept.

Children draw themselves on the front cover to personalise their **Maths Journal**.

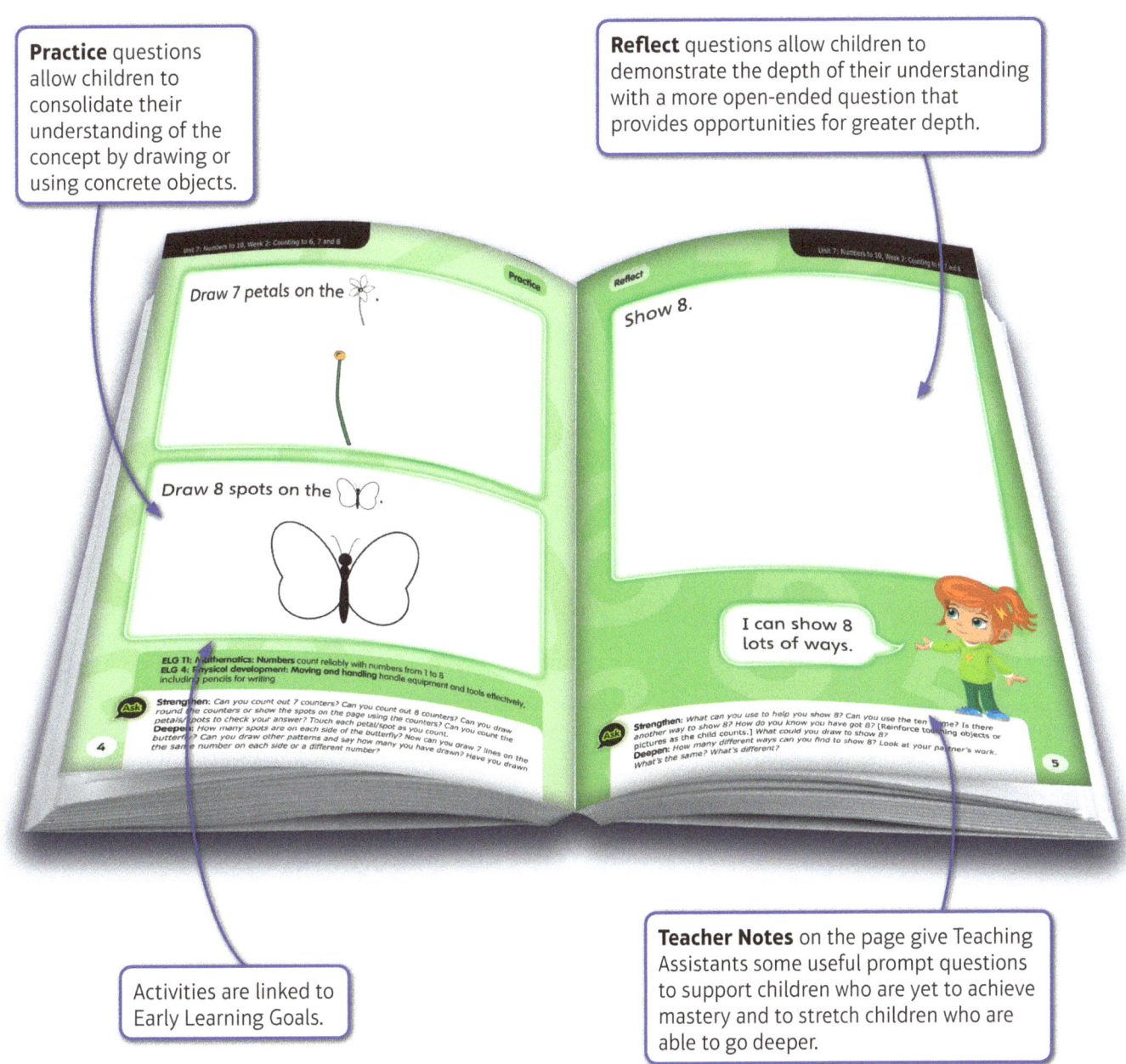

Practice questions allow children to consolidate their understanding of the concept by drawing or using concrete objects.

Reflect questions allow children to demonstrate the depth of their understanding with a more open-ended question that provides opportunities for greater depth.

Activities are linked to Early Learning Goals.

Teacher Notes on the page give Teaching Assistants some useful prompt questions to support children who are yet to achieve mastery and to stretch children who are able to go deeper.

Your *Power Maths Reception* resources

Online subscription

The online subscription gives you access to a variety of helpful resources.

Online Flashcards

The **Online Flashcards** are the starting point for most *Power Maths Reception* lessons. They stimulate children's interest and introduce key mathematical concepts. The flashcards are designed for use on the interactive whiteboard to facilitate either whole class or small group sessions. These taught sessions take around 10–15 minutes per day, and include plenty of hands-on activities.

Teaching tools

From the **Online Flashcards**, you can launch interactive teaching tools that allow you to model and change the structures and representations used in *Power Maths*. This allows you to demonstrate the concept using a variety of examples, to ensure children gain a deep understanding.

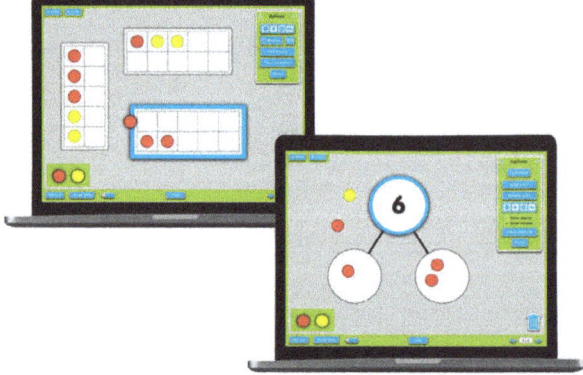

Online versions of Teacher Guide pages

PDF pages give support at both unit and lesson levels.

Mathematical concept videos

Watch the professional development videos as you introduce each new concept to help you teach with confidence. The videos explore how the concept fits in and builds through Reception as well as common misconceptions and how to assess mastery.

What is *Power Maths*?

Created especially for UK primary schools, and aligned with the National Curriculum and the Early Years Framework, *Power Maths* is a whole-class mastery resource that empowers every child to understand and succeed. *Power Maths* rejects the notion that some people simply 'can't do' maths. Instead, it develops growth mindsets and encourages hard work, practice and a willingness to see mistakes as learning tools.

Best practice consistently shows that mastery of small, cumulative steps builds a solid foundation of deep mathematical understanding. *Power Maths* combines interactive teaching tools, high-quality textbooks and continuing professional development (CPD) to help you equip children with a deep and long lasting understanding. Based on extensive evidence, and developed in partnership with practising teachers, *Power Maths* ensures that it meets the needs of children in the UK.

Power Maths and Mastery

Power Maths makes mastery practical and achievable by providing the structures, pathways, content, tools and support you need to make it happen in your classroom.

To develop mastery in maths children need to be enabled to acquire a deep understanding of maths concepts, structures and procedures, step by step. Complex mathematical concepts are built on simpler conceptual components and when children understand every step in the learning sequence, maths becomes transparent and makes logical sense. Interactive lessons establish deep understanding in small steps, as well as effortless fluency in key facts such as counting and number bonds. The whole class works on the same content and no child is left behind.

Power Maths Reception

- Builds every concept in small, progressive steps.
- Combines a mastery approach with Early Years best practice.
- Provides the tools you need to develop growth mindsets.
- Establishes firm foundations for maths learning to enable children to succeed in KS1 and beyond.

The *Power Maths* approach

Everyone can!
Founded on the conviction that every child can achieve, *Power Maths* enables children to build number fluency, confidence and understanding, step by step.

Child-centred learning
Children master concepts one step at a time in lessons that embrace a Concrete-Pictorial-Abstract (C-P-A) approach, avoid overload, build on prior learning and help them see patterns and connections. Same-day intervention ensures sustained progress.

Continuing professional development
Embedded teacher support and development offer every teacher the opportunity to continually improve their subject knowledge and manage whole-class teaching for mastery.

Whole-class teaching
An interactive, whole-class teaching model encourages thinking and precise mathematical language and allows children to deepen their understanding as far as they can.

Introduction

Foreword by the series editor and author, Tony Staneff

For far too long in the UK, maths has been feared by learners – and by many teachers, too. As a result, most learners consistently underachieve. More crucially, negative beliefs about ability, aptitude and the nature of maths are entrenched in children's thinking from an early age.

Yet, as someone who has loved maths all my life, I've always believed that every child has the capacity to succeed in maths. I've also had the great pleasure of leading teams and departments who share that belief and passion. Teaching for mastery, as practised in China and other South-East Asian jurisdictions since the 1980s, has confirmed my conviction that maths really is for everyone and not just those who have a special talent. In recent years, my team and I at Trinity Academy, Halifax, have had the privilege of researching with and working alongside some of the finest mastery practitioners from the UK and beyond, whose impact on learners' confidence, achievement and attitude is an inspiration.

The mastery approach recognises the value of developing the power to think rather than just do. It also recognises the value of making a coherent journey in which whole-class groups tackle concepts in very small steps, one by one. You cannot build securely on loose foundations – and it is just the same with maths: by creating a solid foundation of deep understanding, our children's skills and confidence will be strong and secure. What's more, the mindset of learner and teacher alike is fundamental: everyone can do maths … EVERYONE CAN!

I am proud to have been part of the extensive team responsible for turning the best of the world's practice, research, insights, and shared experiences into *Power Maths*, a unique teaching and learning resource developed especially for UK classrooms. *Power Maths* embodies our vision to help and support primary and Early Years teachers to transform every child's mathematical and personal development. 'Everyone can!' has become our mantra and our passion, and we hope it will be yours, too.

Now, explore and enjoy all the resources you need to teach for mastery, and please get back to us with your *Power Maths* experiences and stories!

Meet the authors

Tony Staneff, Series Editor

Vice Principal at Trinity Academy, Halifax, Tony also leads a team of mastery experts who help schools across the UK to develop teaching for mastery via nationally recognised CPD courses, problem-solving and reasoning resources, schemes of work, assessment materials and other tools.

+ A team of experienced authors, including:

 White Rose Maths (Michael Gosling CEO, Tony Staneff, Beth Smith, Caroline Hamilton, Faye Hirst, Jane Brown and Amy How)

 Beth Smith, Katie Williams, Faye Hirst and Caroline Hamilton – Mastery Specialists with expertise in Early Years

+ A group of teachers and maths co-ordinators

We have consulted our teacher group throughout the development of *Power Maths Reception* to ensure we are meeting their real needs in the classroom.

Photocopiable 1: Number 6	page 102
Photocopiable 2: Number 7	page 103
Photocopiable 3: Number 8	page 104
Photocopiable 4: Number 9	page 105
Photocopiable 5: Number 10	page 106
Photocopiable 6: Ten frame	page 107
Photocopiable 7: Part-whole model	page 108
Photocopiable 8: Butterfly template	page 109
Photocopiable 9: Ladybird template	page 110
Photocopiable 10: Action cards	page 111
Photocopiable 11: Small part-whole models	page 112
Photocopiable 12: Positional language	page 113
Photocopiable 13: Arrow	page 114
Photocopiable 14: 3D shapes	page 115
Photocopiable 15: 2D shapes	page 116
Photocopiable 16: 2D shapes in the environment	page 117
List of practical resources	page 118

Contents

Introduction and Meet the authors	page 4
What is *Power Maths*?	page 5
Your *Power Maths Reception* resources	page 6
Power Maths Reception, yearly overview	page 9
Teaching sequence	page 12
Day 1: Weekly starter	page 13
Day 2: Discover and Share	page 14
Day 3: Think together and Practice	page 15
Day 4: Challenge and Strengthen	page 16
Day 5: Practical activities and Reflect	page 17
Structures and representations	page 18
Applying the C-P-A approach in Reception	page 19
The *Power Maths* characters	page 20
Mathematical language	page 21
Keeping the class together	page 22
Variation helps visualisation	page 23

Unit 6 – Numbers bonds within 5 — page 24
Week 1 – Introducing the part-whole model — page 26

Unit 7 – Numbers to 10 — page 32
Week 2 – Counting to 6, 7 and 8 — page 34
Week 3 – Counting to 9 and 10 — page 40

Unit 8 – Comparing numbers within 10 — page 46
Week 4 – Comparing groups up to 10 — page 48

Unit 9 – Addition to 10 — page 54
Week 5 – Combining 2 groups to find the whole — page 56

Unit 10 – Number bonds to 10 — page 62
Week 6 – Using a ten frame — page 64
Week 7 – The part-whole model to 10 — page 70

Unit 11 – Shape and space — page 76
Week 8 – Spatial awareness — page 78
Week 9 – 3D shapes — page 84
Week 10 – 2D shapes — page 90

Unit 6 Observation sheet	page 96
Unit 7 Observation sheet	page 97
Unit 8 Observation sheet	page 98
Unit 9 Observation sheet	page 99
Unit 10 Observation sheet	page 100
Unit 11 Observation sheet	page 101

Reception Teacher Guide B

A Guide to Teaching for Mastery

Series Editor: Tony Staneff